RECLAIMING
CONSERVATISM

Also by Mickey Edwards

Winning the Influence Game:
What Every Business Leader Should Know about Government
(with Michael Watkins and Usha Thakrar)

Behind Enemy Lines:
A Rebel in Congress Proposes a Bold New Politics for the 1980s

Hazardous to Your Health:
A New Look at the Health Care Crisis in America

RECLAIMING CONSERVATISM

*How a Great American Political Movement Got Lost
—and How It Can Find Its Way Back*

MICKEY EDWARDS

UNIVERSITY PRESS

2008

OXFORD
UNIVERSITY PRESS

Oxford University Press, Inc., publishes works that further
Oxford University's objective of excellence
in research, scholarship, and education.

Oxford   New York
Auckland   Cape Town   Dar es Salaam   Hong Kong   Karachi
Kuala Lumpur   Madrid   Melbourne   Mexico City   Nairobi
New Delhi   Shanghai   Taipei   Toronto

With offices in
Argentina   Austria   Brazil   Chile   Czech Republic   France   Greece
Guatemala   Hungary   Italy   Japan   Poland   Portugal   Singapore
South Korea   Switzerland   Thailand   Turkey   Ukraine   Vietnam

Published by Oxford University Press, Inc.
198 Madison Avenue, New York, New York 10016

www.oup.com

Oxford is a registered trademark of Oxford University Press

Library of Congress Cataloging-in-Publication Data
Edwards, Mickey, 1937–
Reclaiming conservatism : how a great American political movement
got lost—and how it can find its way back / Mickey Edwards.
p.   cm.
ISBN 978-0-19-533558-3
1. Conservatism—United States.   2. Republican Party (U.S. : 1854–)—History—21st century.
3. Executive-legislative relations—United States—History—21st century.
4. United States—Politics and government—2001–   I. Title.
JC573.2.U6E38 2008
320.520973—dc22   2007037166

1 3 5 7 9 8 6 4 2

Printed in the United States of America
on acid-free paper

For Elizabeth

There can be no rebuilding
without rebuilding memory.
—Yevgeny Yevtushenko

Take up the song;
forget the epitaph.
—Edna St. Vincent Millay

CONTENTS

I

THE CONSERVATIVE SOUL

A BAD DAY ON THE HILL

Wゴ ITH its gleaming marble, its chandeliers, its wide corridors, and its spacious offices, there is an imposing air to the Rayburn House Office Building. In the rooms where congressional committees meet to take public testimony and debate proposed legislation, members sit at long, curved tables of polished wood beneath oil portraits of former committee chairmen. This is the seat of the legislative branch—the "first" branch—of American government. The building is meant to convey a sense of majesty, but majesty of a kind different from that symbolized by robes and thrones and jeweled crowns. What is enthroned here is the will of the people.

Just after ten o'clock on the morning of Wednesday, January 31, 2007—less than one month after Democrats, in the minority for more than a decade, resumed control of the House of Representatives—the new chairman of the House Judiciary Committee, John Conyers of Michigan, gathered his committee's members in room 2141 of the Rayburn Building for the first, and potentially the most important, public hearing of his chairmanship. Rows of chairs lined the crowded room, facing the elevated platforms at which the members sat. Except on the rarest of occasions, Congress meets in public, and its hearing rooms are often filled with interested parties, reporters, and members of the general public who are curious to see their government at work. Facing the assembled committee members is a table at which sit expert witnesses called upon to present their views on the issues that form the day's agenda. Even in these days of electronic transcribing and video recording, a courtroom-style stenographer sits at the end of the table, taking down every word, creating a public record of everything that is said. The entire arrangement is designed to send a clear message that this is a place of serious business.

The majority of the seats along the elevated platform were filled that January morning by Democrats, since the party in the majority gets to decide how committee memberships will be apportioned and always gives itself an advantage. The Republican members of the committee, most of whom had become accustomed to the agenda-setting perquisites of legislative dominance, could not have been expected to be happy about finding themselves in the minority, but the matter under consideration was one that should have united the two parties. What Conyers had proposed for that morning was a public hearing to investigate assertions from the White House that presidents, even after they had signed legislative acts into law, could nonetheless unilaterally declare that they had the right not to obey the laws their own signatures had created.

Embodied in a series of "presidential signing statements," these declarations were not partisan in nature. Indeed, the best-known example was a presidential assertion of the right to disregard a congressional ban on the torture of prisoners of war, a prohibition originally sponsored and promoted by Arizona's senior Republican senator, John McCain, a vocal supporter of the president's Iraq war policies. As President Bush used them, signing statements were not merely expressions of opinion; they were direct challenges to the constitutional authority of Congress to determine the law. And every member of the Judiciary Committee, regardless of party affiliation, had taken an oath to uphold the Constitution and to fulfill the duties constitutionally assigned to the legislative branch of the federal government, including, as the people's representatives, the duty to determine the nation's laws.

The previous year, both the Constitution Project and the American Bar Association had formed task forces to look into the president's claims that he had an inherent authority to "interpret" the laws in such a way as to not be bound by them. The task forces included conservatives—among them, current and former national chairmen of the American Conservative Union (the country's largest grassroots conservative organization), former Republican Justice Department officials, and a former FBI director in the administrations of both President Reagan and President Bush's father—as well as prominent Democrats and legal scholars not aligned publicly with either political party.

To ensure that the people's representatives will have the final say in writing the laws, Article 1, Section 7, of the Constitution gives a president only two options in the event that he disagrees with an act of Congress. He may sign it, despite his reservations, in which case it will become law, and thus binding on him as well as on all other Americans. Or he may refuse to sign it and send it back to Capitol Hill, in which case Congress may attempt to override his veto and—if it can gather the necessary two-thirds majorities in both the House and the Senate—impose the legislation as law regardless of his objections.

Both the Constitution Project and Bar Association task forces *unanimously* condemned President Bush's use of signing statements rather than vetoes, which Congress could challenge, as a clear violation of the Constitution. At its 2006 annual meeting, the 550 members of the Bar Association's House of Delegates, representing more than four hundred thousand attorneys, overwhelmingly adopted a statement denouncing the way the president was using signing statements as "contrary to the rule of law and our constitutional system of the separation of powers."

Thus what Conyers was putting before the committee that morning was not some liberal big-government proposal or some challenge to traditional Republican Party policy positions. He was merely asking the committee to resist what appeared to be a clearly unconstitutional expansion of presidential authority—a position that earlier generations of conservatives would have eagerly embraced as their own cause. Indeed, conservatives had long positioned themselves as supporters of a "strict construction" of the Constitution. And that was precisely the issue here.

Although most of the Republican committee members would have described themselves as conservatives and would have been thought of as such by others, their response to the hearing was something no earlier conservative would have recognized as conservative at all. One by one, beginning with the ranking (senior) Republican member of the committee, Lamar Smith of Texas, and the committee's previous chairman, James Sensenbrenner of Wisconsin, they issued a succession of dismissive statements that simply shrugged off the concerns and said, in essence, "What's the big deal?"

One conservative member of the committee, Dan Lungren, a former California attorney general, asked why it wasn't a good thing that at least the president was expressing his opinions of legislation openly, rather than keeping his reservations to himself.

The answer, a point the conservative committee members persisted in ignoring, was that no previous president of either party had ever used the strategy as broadly, or as often, or with such serious potential effect, as had President Bush. These were not merely statements of "opinion"; in more than eleven hundred specific instances—more than all previous presidents combined—the president had challenged portions of the very laws he had just signed, indicating that he considered them not to be binding on himself, on other White House officials, or on any of the departments and agencies of the federal government. Not only was he declaring himself free to ignore the law, he was also asserting a theory of a "unitary" executive branch of government, operating under his authority alone and under which federal agencies could simply ignore legislative requirements that they report to Congress on the status of federal programs that Congress had created and funded—a direct repudiation of any obligation to be held accountable to the peoples' representatives.

Simply put, the president was claiming that a president and the entire executive branch of government had the right, if a president so decided, to disobey the law—an assertion that, if left unchallenged, would establish a dangerous precedent to be followed by any future president determined to ignore any future law. But it was not merely a matter of setting a precedent: in June 2007, the government's General Accounting Office released the findings from a review of agency compliance with just the provisions in fiscal year 2006 appropriations bills. In eleven such signing statements, the president had stated his disagreement with 160 separate provisions of the law. The GAO picked out nineteen of the 160 for review and found that in six of the nineteen—nearly one-third—the federal agencies had indeed ignored the law. It was a random survey, conducted at the request of a Senate committee, but if the ratio held true for the remaining provisions as well, it is likely that federal agencies, in response to the president's directives, may have disobeyed the law more than fifty times in just one year's appropriations bills, a tiny fraction of the administration's declarations that it was free to ignore laws it didn't like.

By the end of that day's hearing, however, not one of the conservatives on the committee had expressed even the slightest discomfort with the idea that a president could simply ignore the law. Historically, conservatives had been skeptical of government and particularly skeptical of its ability to keep its hunger for authority within proper constitutional bounds. Government officials—whether

members of Congress, state officials, local aldermen, or presidents—
are as susceptible to self-aggrandizement as anybody else. Conservatives had always understood that a president had no more right to
simply disobey the law than does the guy who cleans the windshield
at the local filling station. Yet what I heard that day, in that committee room, was nothing less than the quiet rustle of a collective
shrugging of shoulders.

I was a member of the panel called to testify before the Judiciary
Committee. By the end of the day, I was frustrated and angry. As a
lifelong conservative, I had struggled throughout a sixteen-year
congressional career against a liberal majority that often abused its
power, and I had become quite used to viewing those on the other
side of the political aisle as honest, sincere, and well-meaning, but
nonetheless a serious threat to constitutionally limited government.
But with every passing moment in that committee meeting it became clearer to me that it was now Republican "conservatives," my
friends and allies for forty years, who were posing the greatest threat
to the Constitution and its myriad protections.

"What matters," I said angrily, "is whether or not a president
can . . . assert that he does not have to comply with an act of
Congress that has been signed into law . . . this is about the Constitution, and the Constitution is more important than . . . our
party." My comments, which came after five hours of being appalled by what I was witnessing, were broadcast on news reports the
following day. Conservatives who had been present with me at the
movement's founding called to say they agreed with me: what was
now called "conservatism" had become unrecognizable to them,
too.

In *The Conscience of a Conservative*, the book that launched the modern American conservative movement, Barry Goldwater posed the
question he thought should be at the heart of any policy consideration: "Does it maximize freedom?" By January 31, 2007, that

fundamental tenet of American conservatism had apparently been replaced by a very different question: Would criticism of this extra-constitutional assertion of White House supremacy be good or bad, politically, for Republicans? For years, conservative activists had asserted that their constitutional principles, not allegiance to any particular political party, came first; that the Republican Party was merely, at the time, the best available vehicle to try to carry conservative principles into the world of public policy. When I first ran for Congress, even though I was a member of the American Conservative Union's board of directors, the Conservative Victory Fund declined to contribute to my campaign because the Democratic incumbent I was challenging had often voted with conservatives. What mattered was how a legislator voted, not which party he belonged to. To its credit, that organization continues to support conservative Democrats, but by the beginning of 2007, many of the people who called themselves conservatives had apparently become Republicans only, their prescriptions stripped of any principle higher than party unity.

By the time the nation's voters went to the polls in November of 2006, a large number of political observers—and, apparently, ordinary voters as well—had taken note of how extremely dysfunctional the Republican-dominated Congress had become in the half-dozen years since George W. Bush had become president of the United States. In that relatively short time, Congress—the branch that is most directly accountable to the people—had been nearly destroyed as a separate, independent, and equal institution. It seemed to many to have become a virtual rubber stamp for a president who himself seemed to have very little interest in maintaining even the slightest pretense of adherence to the Constitution's system of separated powers.

At the same time, a number of other observers, many of them longtime conservative activists, were lamenting the fact that the people who call themselves "conservatives" today bear very little resemblance to those limited-government advocates who had given birth to the modern conservative movement and had helped shape the modern Republican Party's political agenda.

For most, these two issues—the disturbing transformation of conservative politics and the near-destruction of the United States Congress—seemed distinct and separate. But they were not. Congress had become what it was for those six years, a weak and barely functioning institution, precisely because conservatives had become what they are now—highly partisan activists almost utterly devoid of any governing principle greater than maintaining power and using the considerable weight of their high public positions to impose their personal ideologies over areas of private life that properly lie far outside any constitutional grant of federal authority.

It's not merely a matter of what this strange new breed of state-power Republican "conservatives" had done to Congress; while the Democrats who took over in 2007 may be no better and may even be worse, for now, at least, conservatives are no longer responsible for undermining Congress. But unfortunately the problem goes much deeper and is far more troubling. The incompetence so widely noted during the years of conservative leadership was less serious a matter than was the complete abandonment of principle that marked nearly every day of the single-party Republican dominance of both Congress and the White House for six very long years.

On Capitol Hill, Congress acted as though its top priority was party unity, demonstrated in the form of an almost abject subservience to the head of a constitutionally separate branch of government. At the other end of Pennsylvania Avenue, in the White House, the president, who called himself (and was called by others) a conservative, had become the very embodiment of everything conservatives had long feared and warned against. Operating almost unchecked by any other branch of government, he ordered wiretaps on citizens' phones, held prisoners without trial or charges, and refused to provide information to Congress even when federal law required him to do so. For nearly half a century, conservatives had worried that a leftist president, if given the opportunity, might do such things. Now those things were being done by a man who called himself a "conservative," and "conservatives" cheered him on. Those who once had wanted only that the government leave them alone as much as possible, who once had warned of the dangers of Big Brother, had created the monster government they most feared.

I have spent more than forty years being a part of the American conservative movement, beginning as a participant in the early stages of the conservative takeover of the Republican establishment, with the election of a Goldwater supporter to the Young Republican national chairmanship in the summer of 1963, and eventually serving as the national chairman of the American Conservative Union, chairing the annual Conservative Political Action Conferences in Washington, and becoming one of the three founding trustees of the Heritage Foundation. I wrote this book because the political movement that I helped to create as a leader in the conservative movement is now in the process of destroying everything it had once professed to believe in. Indeed, much of what I see described as "conservatism" today seems strikingly similar to those policies and attitudes *against* which that movement was directed.

This change in conservatism has been striking not only in the presidency, with its broad claims to "inherent" powers, but also in Congress, the institution through which the people exercise a collective control over public policy and national priorities. If Congress is silenced, the people themselves are silenced. Indeed, the Constitution, which has for more than two and a quarter centuries served as the chief guarantor of our liberties, is silenced. If the Constitution is silenced, and if it is "conservatives" who have been instrumental in silencing it, then the limited-government conservatism I have known is dead and American democracy itself is at risk.

Though there are beneficial aspects to government's ability to marshal society's resources, we must remain aware of the dangers an overly muscular government can pose. In Taylor Caldwell's book *Great Lion of God*, Joseph says to Saul, "Was it not the Chinese who declared that governments are more to be feared than a tiger?" History has clearly demonstrated the immense and often fatal consequences of living in a society in which the power of the state can be brought to bear to oppress, directly or indirectly, those who are not part of the approved mainstream. Could be Jews. Could be Catholics. Could be gays. Could be liberals. Could be Gypsies. Could, in fact, be almost anybody who is not part of a society's momentary majority. Bottom line: Too much government can be bad for your health. If you don't believe it, remember that the big government of today in our country can read your mail, listen to your phone calls, read your bank records, watch your car as it moves through city streets, keep tabs on the books you check out of the library—and it has done so without a court order that would at least require some serious proof of the urgent public need to do so.

Conservatives believed, first, in limiting the reach of government (a position that required nothing more dramatic than simply supporting and adhering to constitutional constraints on government power). It was Senator Goldwater who observed that any government big enough to give you everything you want is also big enough to take everything you have. Sound like an absurd exaggeration? An oversimplification? Not if you read history.

Second, the conservatism I signed on for emphasized the dignity of the individual person; it was, in final analysis, the human being, not the collective, that mattered the most. That didn't preclude group pride or group identity or even the occasionally necessary groupings for purposes of public policy, but conservatives cared more about individuals than about collectives. It's one of the big differences between conservatives and liberals. I respect both, and I certainly understand a primary emphasis on groupings (it's clearly easier to address endemic problems if one thinks of the problems as common to people of a certain defining characteristic). But I fell on the side of those whose principal concern was the person, not "the people." In Aleksandr Solzhenitsyn's novel *Cancer Ward*, the Russian bureaucrat Rusanov, diagnosed with cancer and sent to a hospital ward, is soon uncomfortable with all the sick and complaining people around him. "The Rusanovs loved the People, their great People," Solzhenitsyn wrote. "They served the People and were ready to give their lives for the People. But as the years went by they found themselves less and less able to tolerate actual human beings." Perhaps groupthink is better for theory than for life. Theodore Roszak, describing Karl Marx, observed that "there is no sensitivity for the person—only for the people." I prefer people to The People.

Third, conservatism once stood for liberty. Liberty, in fact, and especially the liberty emphasized in America's founding documents, was not granted by the state (in which case the state could, when it chose, rescind the grant); it preceded the state. This was a liberty that was focused on the rights of the people, not the authority of governments; that recognized that the people had created the government, not the other way around; that they had created governments for their common protection, not to empower a few in high office to mold society to their liking; that government had what rights the people gave it, not the reverse.

I am not a libertarian in the purist sense. I believe there are important roles for government, but like many conservatives I believe in a government constrained by certain fundamental and overarching principles, and in a framework that holds those principles in place: the diffusion and balancing of governmental powers and an unassailable system to protect the individual liberties of the American people.

Finally, I am a conservative because conservatives at one time believed strongly in the creation of opportunity. It was not equality of outcome that mattered so much as a determination to protect each citizen's opportunity to go as far as possible beyond the point at which his or her parents had left off. There are those, of course, who will dispute this point, who will argue that conservative resistance to attempts at "leveling" actually serves to block, not enhance, opportunity. But we conservatives believed that so long as society provided a fair safety net for those who were unable to care for themselves, if taxation and regulation were kept in reasonable bounds and artificial barriers to advancement were removed, individuals would have a chance to go as far as their talents and energies and perseverance could take them. The goal was not to maintain subsistence just beyond the poverty level but to provide an open door for citizens to achieve their own prosperity.

My grandparents all came from an oppressive Europe. Had they remained in Europe they would have very likely continued along the same narrow path, generation after generation (at least until the time came when a pogrom or a Holocaust swallowed them up). Instead, they came to America. Though the streets here were not paved with gold, they were paved with golden opportunities. Here immigrants could start on a different cycle, one that moved upward, not in circles. So it was in my family. One of my grandfathers scratched out a living by selling rags from a cart he pushed through the streets of Cleveland; the other earned a small living as a worker in a scrap metal yard. My father grew up in an orphanage; neither of my parents went to college. As a young man, my father got a job selling shoes and, by working six days and six nights a week, eventually became a store manager (a job in which he continued to work the same long hours). My mother, too, worked six days and six nights a week, as a bookkeeper during the day and in the shoe store at night. As a result, my parents, who had little, were better off, financially, than their parents, who had very little indeed. I have been more successful still, though I would not pretend to be half the man my father was or nearly the equal of my mother. On the day I was sworn in as a member of Congress, my mother said to me, "Who are we to have a member of Congress in our family?" It was a good question. Who were we? We were people whose parents had come to an America of freedom and opportunity.

It is these things—the love of freedom and opportunity and the dignity of every individual—that were the soul of American conservatism. This book is about reclaiming that soul. And that begins with the Constitution.

Many, and conservatives in particular, like to talk of American "exceptionalism," but it is the Constitution, not military or economic power, that makes America exceptional. Over the course of some forty years, the conservative movement has been transformed from the single most forceful, and most consistent, defender of the Constitution to its most dangerous opponent. Once the most ardent champions of the Constitution's deliberately constructed system of circumscribed and constrained federal power, conservatives have discarded the framework as though it were merely an obstruction to imposing on society their own views of a utopian world.

This book will both map the evolution in conservative thought (or, rather, the gradual misappropriation of the conservative label) and show why what was founded as a movement to maximize freedom and respect individual choice has come instead to be a campaign for partisan advantage and a decidedly nonconservative ideology. This book is about a very real, and very serious, threat to American liberties, promulgated under the cover of the conservative name. It is a story of how we "conservatives" have moved from Barry Goldwater and the love of freedom to wiretaps, secret prisons, government intrusion into the most intimate private decisions, and the unprecedented assertion of federal authority and a presidency and bureaucracy that places itself above the law. The movement that once championed strict limits on federal power now recognizes virtually no limits at all. This book will be about how that came to be, how conservatism has become the enemy of all it once stood for and about what must be done to take the movement back from those who have stolen it.

In his book *In Defence of Politics*, the British political theorist Bernard Crick wrote that "politics is the way a free people govern themselves." Politics—engagement in the shaping of one's society—is among the most noble of all human endeavors. A politics that sets aside concerns about principle or cedes the defining of principle to others, or that holds to no principle greater than the mere retention of political power or imposition of one's beliefs on others, is an affront not only to the society in which it is found but to the very concept of self-government.

Two caveats are in order. First, although I was an active participant in the development of modern American conservatism, I am not a trained historian, and I will not trace in minute detail the personalities and conflicts that shaped the movement that succeeded in nominating Barry Goldwater for president and later elected Ronald Reagan. That story has been told many times and several of the best accounts are included in the suggested readings at the conclusion of this book. My concern is not the structure of the movement or its most prominent adherents but its core beliefs, for it is those beliefs that have been distorted. I have been struck as I wrote this book by how long the disintegration of American conservatism has been unfolding. We did not come to this point quickly and reclaiming it will not happen overnight.

Second, this book is not only about conservatism. It is also a book about the Constitution and therefore at least as much about James Madison and the nation's founders as about a Barry Goldwater or a Ronald Reagan. If American conservatism were merely another political force undergoing transformation—if conservatives were nothing more than the Whigs of the twenty-first century—the changes would simply form the fodder for an article in a political science journal. The fact, simple and inescapable—and very frightening—is that many of today's conservatives simply don't care at all what the Constitution says. This book is about the nexus between twenty-first-century conservatism and the nation's current constitutional crisis, for which today's conservatives are largely to blame.

Forty years ago, we conservatives began our slow climb to political dominance. Today we can see what we have become—what we have built and what we have destroyed. In the musical version of *Les Misérables*, the drunken Thenardier's wife recalls their courtship and moans: "God almighty, have you seen what's happened since?" It's a good question. Conservatives began a courtship with the American people with a pledge to champion the freedoms and opportunities made possible by the unique document that limited the government and put its faith in the people. That was the "soul" of conservatism when it had a soul. But have you seen what's happened since?

THE BIRTH OF MODERN CONSERVATISM

American political conservatism had many antecedents. In what former Secretary of Defense Donald Rumsfeld called the "old Europe," political "conservatives" were the establishmentarians who supported the most traditional means of governance: monarchs, nobles, wealthy landlords, powerful churches. Conservatism was a philosophy of ruling classes and class distinctions, of the rulers (the "deciders") and the ruled, of centralized and sometimes absolute authority, and of the powerless masses whose lives were shaped by the decrees of others.

During that time, however, a revolutionary new perspective emerged and slowly became increasingly powerful. In the seventeenth century, building on the Magna Carta and other early documents that had attempted over many years, with mixed results, to rein in the arbitrary rule of British kings, John Locke agitated for recognition of important and fundamental rights which attached to every citizen at birth and could not be arbitrarily denied. A century later, in France, an aroused citizenry, chafing under the intolerable excesses of a profligate ruling class and a capricious king, embarked on a path that would before long lead to a bloody revolution. For nearly six hundred years, in small steps and large, a movement grew that had as its common theme a check on arbitrary rule and, as Locke had urged, a new assertion of the inherent rights—the divine rights—not of kings but of individual citizens. This was the birth of the modern liberal idea. And across the Atlantic, it was to provide the philosophical underpinning of the new American state.

In his four-volume treatise *The Wisdom of Conservatism*, Peter Witonski cites kings, popes, and poets; Cicero (defender of aristocracy) and Machiavelli; King James I ("As it is atheism and blasphemy to dispute what God can do, so it is presumption and high contempt in a subject to dispute what a king can") and Metternich (who dismissed self-government as "moral gangrene"). In October 1946, in a speech to a Conservative Party conference, Winston Churchill said, "Our main objectives are: To uphold the Christian religion and resist all attacks upon it" (a far cry from the American constitutional model which proclaims a strict neutrality as to matters of religion) "and to defend our Monarchical and Parliamentary Constitution" (the American system is decidedly antimonarchy and creates a governing structure in which legislative and executive functions are deliberately separated, whereas the parliamentary system just as deliberately combines them). Clearly, what had been created in America was quite different from what had gone before. In America, there was something new to be "conserved" and protected.

In the American colonies, Thomas Jefferson articulated the right of citizens to throw off the increasingly oppressive rule of a distant king and argued for a recognition of certain citizen rights that were properly beyond the reach of any king, whether distant or near; more than a decade later, his ally, James Madison, led the effort to create a new federal constitution that gave the national government (a government selected by the people themselves!) sufficient authority to sustain itself but nonetheless placed important powers beyond the reach of government. Even many of those powers that were specifically delegated to the national government were divided and subdivided and parceled out to separate and competing circles of authority to prevent any ambitious person (a would-be Napoleon) from gathering too much power into his own hands.

But still it was not enough: two other Virginians, Patrick Henry and George Mason, insisted that this new constitution, which had inarguably placed considerable powers in the hands of the central government—far more than had existed in the earlier Articles of Confederation—also contain a clear and unambiguous expression of their new nation's commitment to those individual and inviolable liberties whose existence Thomas Jefferson had earlier touched upon in the Declaration of Independence. And then, for fear that future would-be tyrants might wrongly conclude that the citizens retained only those specific rights that were singly enumerated—freedom of religion, freedom of the press, right to assemble, right to petition the government, and so on—they added, and the states ratified, both the Ninth and Tenth Amendments, whose purpose was to reiterate and underscore the clear intention of the founders that any rights not specifically delegated to the federal government and not mentioned in the first eight amendments remained with the people or the states, not the federal government. It was, simply, a take-no-chances declaration limiting the scope of government authority, the ultimate result of centuries of accumulated grievance and a growing determination of the people to free themselves from the rule of others.

The Constitution is the apotheosis of political liberalism, and it was reverence for this document, and resistance to those in government who would seek to expand their powers beyond those the Constitution granted, that led to the rise of the modern conservative movement in the United States. The political movement that gained its strength incrementally but continually after the presidential election of 1964, was a distinctly *American* style of conservatism.

What it sought to conserve was not the authority of rulers or churches or powerful landlords, but a framework with an emphasis on the rights of the individual citizen.

These people—these *conservers* of the limits established by the Constitution—were known as conservatives. In some sense, of course, they were conserving tradition. However, it was not *ancient* tradition but the revolutionary new concepts of human freedom, embodied in the Constitution, that they were dedicated to preserving. America's founders were revolutionaries not merely in the military sense, breaking violently away from the British monarchy that had so arbitrarily circumscribed their rights; they were revolutionaries ideologically as well, breaking away from the very ideas of monarchy, aristocracy, state-sponsored religion, and centralized government authority. It would have been more accurate to describe this new and distinctly American conservative—supporter of history's most revolutionary constitution—as a political first cousin to the traditional European liberal, the political descendants of John Locke. Theirs was a very different political perspective than that being advocated by supporters of a more centralized, and more directive, government, who had now somehow become known, in a strange American twist of the language, as "liberals." In fact, many of American conservatism's most prominent spokesmen, such as the renowned economist Friedrich Hayek, a leading proponent of limited government and free-market capitalism, insisted throughout their lives on describing themselves as "classical liberals," a historically more accurate description of what an American conservative really was. Keeping government in check was not only the primary ingredient of the Lockean and Madisonian liberalism that lay at the heart of America's founding document; it was also the key element defining what a truly American conservatism was all about.

Barry Goldwater had made conservatism's central concern clear in his 1964 speech accepting the Republican presidential nomination in San Francisco's Cow Palace arena. "Extremism in the defense of liberty," Goldwater said, "is no vice." By definition, of course, extremism *is* a vice, and what Goldwater clearly meant to say was that a strong and unwavering commitment to the defense of personal liberties is an absolute essential in a world in which government increasingly encroached into citizens' lives. In fact, Goldwater's concept of good government was more accurately summed up in the second (and often forgotten) half of that famous sentence: "moderation in the pursuit of justice is no virtue." (Unfortunately, however, the actual words used to convey his views had been written not by Goldwater himself but by a campaign speechwriter named Karl Hess. At the end of a letter he wrote to me after Goldwater's defeat, Hess added a handwritten note. "Remember," he wrote, "the enemy is the State." This was, in fact, a giant leap beyond anything Goldwater, who spent more than thirty years as a part of "the State," would have believed or subscribed to.)

Conservative thought in America did not begin with Barry Goldwater, of course, but Goldwater's conservatism was a considerable departure from what had passed for conservatism before his arrival on the political scene. One may have had socially conservative values—the kind that led one to attend church or synagogue, to keep one's lawn and bushes well trimmed, to dress modestly, spend frugally, and drive within the established speed limit. (Witonski called this "a style of thinking . . . about all aspects of life and civilization." It may refer, he said, "to certain elementary prejudices in taste and habit, such as a tendency to dress traditionally.") Whatever this "style of thinking" was, it wasn't something that set hearts aflame. It was lifestyle conservatism, not a political conservatism, and certainly not any kind of political "movement."

In post–World War II America, there was a palpable desire for a return to a kind of comfortable normalcy and, as described in Sloan Wilson's novel *The Man in the Gray Flannel Suit*, a strong tendency toward conformity. There was no serious or widespread political or cultural revolution under way, neither against the growing government bureaucracy nor against concentrated capital, nor even against the continued segregation, discrimination, and oppressive treatment of minorities. In this sense, America was "conservative" primarily in the sense that most American citizens quietly accepted the status quo.

Pre-Goldwater conservatism was a far cry from what it became with his nomination and its appeal to the young insurgents who reshaped the conservative landscape, built a political movement, and transformed, for decades, the Republican Party. Goldwater didn't create this new movement on his own, but his was a different, and movement-shaping, voice. For example, William F. Buckley Jr., the founder of the *National Review*, played a leading role in winning recognition—and some credibility—for conservative views, but despite his support of Goldwater's presidential campaign, his arguments were less about protecting citizen rights than about the centrality of capitalism and the church. Russell Kirk, less well known nationally but prominent among conservative intellectuals, argued that conservatism rested on a foundation of the church, which he saw as the basis of a "transcendent moral order," and he claimed that society required the existence of social classes. Custom, convention, and tradition lay at the heart of Kirk's "conservatism." Kirk's best-known book was *The Conservative Mind*, in which he set forth his canons of conservative belief, but the most revealing was *The Roots of American Order*, which, as described by the *New York Times*, "traces the roots of American civilization to ancient Jerusalem and Rome."

Frank Meyer, Buckley's associate at *National Review*, shaped a "fusionist" argument that sought to reconcile the more libertarian views of Goldwater's supporters and the "traditionalist" perspectives that dominated Kirk's writings. For a good many years this effort managed to help conservatives of these very different perspectives bridge their differences and form the political coalition that eventually put Ronald Reagan in the White House. But it was clear that there was a deep underlying tension that could not be easily erased. America was not a land built on "custom" and "tradition"; it was a land born in revolution, with a new doctrine emphasizing restrictions on executive prerogative and protections for individual rights. Moreover, it diminished church authority by protecting the proliferation of religious, and even nonreligious, perspectives. And what the founders had established in America was a far cry from the dictatorships of ancient Rome, in which over time monarchs had stripped the elected consuls of power and consolidated authority. What Kirk and other traditionalists offered was a conservatism of a sort but very different from the Constitution- and liberty-centered ideals of a truly American conservatism.

There was one overriding factor in "fusionism's" success in holding competing conservative factions together: the threat posed by the Soviet Union. First under Joseph Stalin and then under a succession of equally confrontational communist leaders, the Soviet Union was rapidly rebuilding its military strength after the devastation of World War II and aggressively expanding its reach beyond the so-called captive nations of eastern Europe. America lived in a constant state of awareness that war with the Soviets was a very real possibility and that in a nuclear age such a war might well destroy not just this country but possibly the entire world. The Soviet Union seemed in every conceivable way the antithesis of everything America believed in: a highly repressive totalitarian state that had murdered millions of its own citizens and operated on the basis of enforced collectivism. It intended to dominate the world and made no secret of it.

Anticommunism, fueled by a legitimate fear of the Soviet Union and its attempts to spy on and infiltrate U.S. decision-making circles, played a major role in American conservatism from the mid-1940s until the USSR's ultimate collapse half a century later. With very real spy stories in the news (Whittaker Chambers, Alger Hiss, Julius and Ethel Rosenberg), novelists and screenwriters churned out stories pitting Western heroes against Communist bloc villains. Popular television programs such as *I Led Three Lives* detailed efforts by the FBI to block Soviet infiltration. Many Americans were concerned that the government was not doing enough to protect the country against this very committed and very dangerous enemy. The most concerned became the foundational architects of Cold War Republican conservatism, although a good many liberal Democrats, including Presidents Harry Truman, John F. Kennedy, and Lyndon Johnson, and such senators as Henry Jackson of Washington State and Hubert Humphrey of Minnesota, were also vocal proponents of a muscular American response to the threat.

Associated with this altogether reasonable fear and advocacy of a more robust security response was yet another kind of response, a small, fringe, know-nothing twist on conservatism. To nobody's surprise, later evidence from the files of the Soviet Union proved, as Wisconsin Senator Joseph McCarthy had alleged, that the Soviets had indeed planted spies in important positions in the United States. But McCarthy, who was seemingly completely oblivious to—or dismissive of—any American constitutional and legal principles, hurled accusations without proof, brandishing phony lists of supposed traitors and ultimately discrediting his own cause. Robert Welch, a Massachusetts candy maker, formed a new national organization based in the Boston suburb of Belmont called the John Birch Society, which not only saw spies, traitors, and turncoats at every turn, but decided that America's true enemies were not the Soviet Union or the relatively new Communist government in China, but the U.S. Supreme Court and the United Nations. Billboards reading "Impeach Earl Warren" (then the chief justice of the Supreme Court) and "Get the US Out of the UN" began to appear on the nation's highways. It was a time when fanatics railed against enemies both real and imagined and many Americans took the warnings seriously. Ordinary citizens, faced with an aggressively expansionist communism and frightened by the prospect of nuclear war, built bomb shelters in their backyards, stockpiled canned foods, and worried about threats both to freedom and survival. Many found themselves swept up in the fear generated by both the circumstances and the alarmist rhetoric. "A lot of people in my home town have been attracted to the (Birch) society and I am impressed by the people in it," Goldwater said in an April 1961 article in *Time* magazine. To many others, however, conservatism seemed a movement populated by reactionaries.

But a more far-reaching and rational conservatism was also emerging. In 1944, Friedrich Hayek, who was to receive a Nobel Prize for his work, articulated the economic argument that was to form a basis for the kind of political philosophy Goldwater embraced. The Foundation for Economic Education, based in New York, promoted free-market ideas such as Hayek's with its seminars and its pocket-size magazine, *The Freeman*. Hayek's book, *The Road to Serfdom*, was a tremendous success—more than a quarter-million copies were sold, along with six hundred thousand copies of a *Reader's Digest* condensed version—and the intellectually inclined received the book enthusiastically. Nonetheless, neither Hayek nor his teacher and fellow free-market economist Ludwig von Mises had much direct influence on the bulk of the population. Their call for a libertarian economics helped to form a foundation for a political movement, but economic theory on its own was not enough to bring about a change in the direction of American politics.

Thus, what passed for conservatism in the two decades after World War II was a very strange stew made up of a host of disparate ingredients: an aggressively liberal free-market economics; a trimmed-lawn suburbia of Sunday school values; a rational—and sometimes quite irrational—response to a substantial military and ideological threat; a yearning for adherence to a "transcendent moral order" and an overtly sectarian Christian society; and a rant demanding that the United Nations be kicked out of New York and that the chief justice of the Supreme Court be impeached.

Eight years after publication of Hayek's book, a city councilman from the still-small community of Phoenix, Arizona, was elected to the U.S. Senate. Barry Morris Goldwater was both a true and unique creature of the American West. Rugged-looking, square-jawed, a half-Jewish outdoorsman, he was a college dropout most comfortable wearing boots and blue jeans, piloting his own small plane, and taking gallery-quality nature photographs as he hiked through the mesas and canyons of Arizona, where he formed close and lasting friendships with the Indians he visited. Goldwater's native conservatism was altogether different from the old-school big-business eastern seaboard variety and equally unlike the small-business parochial traditionalism of the American Midwest. Goldwater's economic focal point was not corporate profit, though he was in favor of it, but on "free enterprise," an embrace of the market system not merely because it was the most efficient and productive economic system (the rationale offered by many other supporters of capitalism) but because it permitted citizens the greatest freedom to pursue their own ambitions. Goldwater often expressed his distaste for the emerging radical lifestyles of the '60s and '70s, but his was not a lifestyle-centered conservatism, and though he had his opinions and held them strongly, he did not see it as his role to force his preferences on others.

Whereas Russell Kirk had put heavy emphasis on religion, and especially on Christianity, as indispensable to Western civilization, Goldwater emphasized individual choice and believed that each individual citizen was responsible for his or her own spiritual development. Years later, in response to conservatives' attacks on allowing gays to serve in the military, Goldwater, who had been a military pilot, replied that he didn't care whether people in the military were gay or straight so long as they could shoot straight. By that point, Goldwater believed conservatism had fallen prey to a strident homophobia that he viewed as "just plain dumb." Conservatives, Goldwater thought, "should stand for freedom and only freedom," a position viewed as outrageous by many latter-day conservatives, who have become increasingly statist in their desire to have the government mandate codes of conduct they find acceptable. Goldwater didn't mention, but could have, that much of modern conservatism's political success in the years since he won the Republican presidential nomination had been a direct result of the leadership activities of gay conservatives. One of Goldwater's fellow Arizonans, former Congressman Jim Kolbe, who served as chairman of a House Appropriations subcommittee and played a key role in helping fellow Republicans work toward their goal of less, and less expensive, more accountable government, is gay. As is Steve Gunderson, who as a Republican congressman from Wisconsin, served as an effective and articulate deputy party whip. After Jimmy Carter defeated Gerald Ford for the presidency, one of the Republicans who used his considerable mastery of House rules to fight for conservative positions was Robert Bauman, a congressman from Maryland's eastern shore and one of my predecessors as national chairman of the American Conservative Union. Bauman, too, was gay.

In his 2006 book, *Conservatives without Conscience*, John Dean describes a speech to the conservative Philadelphia Society by a woman named Sarah Bramwell, a former senior editor of *National Review*. The speech was remarkable for the way it managed to turn modern American conservatism on its head. Since the 1960s, said Bramwell, the conservative movement "took on a third goal, namely winning the culture wars." By this she meant "everything from preserving traditional morality, to passing on the Western inheritance, to preserving a distinctly American culture." It was as though the Constitution, with its protection of individual differences, no longer existed.

What Goldwater created was the first truly *American* conservatism, grounded not on the prescriptions of a hierarchy of social orders and classes or on a specific religious faith, but rather on religious diversity and on holding public officeholders accountable to the people. This conservatism challenged how one looked at individual citizens. It had become common on the political left to refer to the "common man," meaning the nonelites, the nonwealthy, and the nonpowerful. Goldwater and his supporters bristled at the idea that ordinary citizens might merely be seen as part of a collective mass. It was a central theme of Goldwater conservatism that there was no such thing as a merely "common" man. No matter their circumstances, every man and woman, in conservative eyes, was unique: an individual possessed of a singularity to be respected. It was a rhetorical distinction, but for these new conservatives it was also a real distinction, one that described a very different approach to questions of liberty and individual choice.

Until Goldwater burst dramatically onto the national political scene (in his first race for an office greater than a seat on his local city council, in 1952, he upset the incumbent majority leader of the Senate, Democrat Ernest McFarland), political conservatism had not been much of a factor either in national elections or in setting public policy. There were conservative journals, but they were few in number and had relatively modest circulations—even *National Review* and the newsletter-sized *Human Events* reached only limited audiences. There were conservative newspaper columnists and broadcasters, such as Fulton Lewis Jr. and John Chamberlain, but they were relatively few. And there were not many conservative officeholders—a couple of handfuls of senators and representatives. To many, conservatism seemed a throwback to a world of class distinction, church dominance, and a preference for governance by one's natural superiors. What had *that* to do with America?

This all changed in 1960 with *The Conscience of a Conservative*. The book became a runaway best-seller. Goldwater had served in the Senate for ten years and had attracted a considerable national following. In coverage leading up to the 1964 presidential election, *Time* magazine reported that a survey of its correspondents "indicates that at least one Republican, Barry Goldwater, could give Kennedy a breathlessly close contest."

The specter of a Goldwater campaign was predictably unnerving to a great many members of the Republican establishment. His exuberant new conservatism was a radical departure from both the more staid upper-Midwest variety, represented most notably by the man known as "Mr. Republican" at the time, Senator Robert A. Taft of Ohio, and the East Coast country-club version whose best-known representative was Nelson Rockefeller, then the Republican governor of New York. Swept up by their enthusiasm for Goldwater's stress on individual liberties and governmental limits, his young followers were sharply critical of most of the existing party leadership: Governor William Scranton and Senator Hugh Scott, both of Pennsylvania; Senator Henry Cabot Lodge of Massachusetts; New York Senators Jacob Javits and Kenneth Keating. All were seen as part of a liberal political power elite that spanned both major parties. Goldwater was rocking the political boat in ways that seemed frightening to those who had embraced, or come to terms with, the post–World War II status quo. Goldwater's "libertarian" conservatives were eager to purge the Republican Party of its so-called Rockefeller wing.

The feeling was mutual. An effort was made to derail the Goldwater candidacy—Rockefeller, Scranton, and Michigan Governor George Romney all took a crack at him, and Rockefeller remained a serious challenger until Goldwater defeated him in California's presidential primary—but Goldwater had won the hearts of thousands of committed young activists throughout the country, many of whom were willing to spend countless hours campaigning. In Illinois, Hillary Rodham, later to become Senator Clinton, was a "Goldwater Girl"; in Arizona, so was Sandra Day, later to become Supreme Court Justice O'Connor; in California, the actor Ronald Reagan, who had been the head of the film industry's labor union, moved into Goldwater's camp.

In his 1951 book *The True Believer*, Eric Hoffer described the phenomenon of the "true believer," one who becomes part of a transcendent cause, working for something bigger and more important than oneself. Whether it was out of a need for the self-esteem boost one gets from "belonging" or the result of a deeply felt passion, many young Goldwater enthusiasts were true believers.

When true believers are pitted against weekend warriors, the weekend warriors (or, as Thomas Paine might have called them, "sunshine activists") rarely win. In 1964, many states still selected their delegates to the Republican Party's national convention at their own congressional district or state conventions. Here the highly motivated Goldwater volunteer network came fully into play, winning convention battles across the country and sending delegates to the national convention in San Francisco. By the time the delegates gathered in California, victory was all but certain; the Republican establishment, now in the person of Governor Scranton, made a feeble last-ditch effort to wrest the nomination from the Goldwater forces, but it was over. Barry Goldwater, the champion of an entirely new kind of conservatism, and the man some thought might have been able to defeat John Kennedy, would be the Republican candidate for president.

That "breathlessly close contest" that *Time's* editors had envisioned never happened, of course. After President Kennedy's assassination in November 1963, the election of his successor, the man whom Kennedy had personally chosen to be next in line for the presidency, was a foregone conclusion. Lyndon Johnson defeated Goldwater in what was then the most lopsided presidential election in all of American history. Goldwater supporters could later recognize each other from a distance by the defiant "One in 27 million" bumper stickers they had placed on their cars after the election; those 27 million Goldwater votes accounted for less than 39 percent of the total votes cast.

Many Goldwater supporters believed his defeat was the result of Johnson's success in painting him as a madman likely to trigger a nuclear war (a perception Goldwater played into himself when he suggested using low-grade nuclear material for defoliation of the leafy areas that North Vietnamese fighters used to shield themselves from observation by American aircraft). And it was undoubtedly damaging to the public's image of Goldwater and his supporters when liberals seized on the fact that Kennedy's assassination had taken place in Dallas, a city thought of as a bastion of conservative politics, to imply—and sometimes directly assert—that conservatives were to blame for the killing (even after it became clear that the murder had actually been committed by Lee Harvey Oswald, a pro-Soviet leftist). The truth is that any chance at all of a Goldwater victory disappeared long before the 1964 election campaign even began, on the day that Kennedy, his personal friend and political rival, was shot in Dallas.

Most political observers, noting the landslide proportions of the Goldwater defeat, declared that conservatism was officially dead. But despite the resounding defeat in the 1964 elections, the Goldwater campaign gave birth to the movement that later elected Ronald Reagan and a conservative majority in Congress (columnist George Will later wrote that Goldwater had lost forty-four states but won the future). It was neither Lyndon Johnson nor the American Left that eventually destroyed Goldwater's brand of conservatism. It was the conservatives who followed him.

THE CONSERVATIVE TRANSFORMATION

Barry Goldwater's conception of a new and distinctively American conservatism—one in which the thing being "conserved" was the liberal revolution embodied in the Constitution—energized thousands of young idealists in the 1960s. It was the idea, not the man, that inspired them. The distinction is important because Goldwater himself, blunt and undiplomatic, was often the worst possible champion of the cause he came to represent.

Goldwater's failing, like that of many men and women who become so committed to a cause, was that his foresight could also function as a set of blinders. Goldwater rose to prominence at a time of overreaching government, marked by rapidly increasing federal spending and a bureaucracy that was expanding in size and scope.

For Goldwater, the urgent need to rein in the government, coupled with his keen sense of the limits that the Constitution imposed on government action, established the parameters of his political priorities. But the Constitution in fact provides for both empowerment and constraint: limits on the government's role—limits which Goldwater clearly saw—but also the necessary authority to breathe life into its aspirations.

The Declaration of Independence had justified separation from Great Britain on the grounds that "all men are created equal." The fact that American colonists (who were, themselves, British citizens) were not afforded the rights that were due all Englishmen was seen as sufficient cause for severing ties to the king, the Parliament, and the British people. The declaration's defiant insistence on "unalienable" rights and equality was universally applicable, but eleven years later, when the Constitution was drafted, those supposedly universal sentiments were not universally applied. Although the founders may have aspired to create a nation that guaranteed liberty and equality, if they actually thought of women or men who were not free or were nonwhite as their "equals" there is precious little evidence of it. Nor was there much evidence of it for a great many years afterward. It was thus important for any public figure of our more enlightened age to consider what was required to make the promise a reality.

Goldwater, however, was focused on the founders' other central premise—strict limits on government authority—and he voted against the 1964 Civil Rights Act on the grounds that the Constitution did not permit such federal intrusion into areas of decision-making that were reserved to the states. Goldwater had supported equal rights for minorities in Arizona long before his election to the Senate, but focusing exclusively on what the Constitution was meant to prevent, and not sufficiently on what it was designed to create, and casting a vote at odds with his own character and inclinations damaged both his own reputation and that of the new movement he was so instrumental in creating.

In 1964, Goldwater carried only six states. One was his native state of Arizona, and the other five were all in the Deep South: Louisiana, Mississippi, Alabama, Georgia, and South Carolina—states that then still formed the heart of a disturbingly racist slice of America. In those states, which had long been central to the Democratic Party's national coalition (the Republican Party was so weak in the former Confederacy that winning a Democratic primary victory there was generally considered tantamount to being elected), Goldwater was wrongly seen as an ally in the fight for what Alabama's Democratic governor, George Wallace, described as "segregation today, segregation tomorrow, segregation forever."

Segregation eventually ended, of course, at least legally, and Goldwater conservatives continued to grow in numbers and expand their influence until they became some of the most important strategists in Republican politics. But a parallel "conservative" political universe was taking shape, particularly in the South. Goldwater's focus may have been on the Constitution but Wallace was honing a very different message. Wallace ran for president himself in 1964 and did surprisingly well in several Democratic primaries, especially in Maryland and Wisconsin, winning as much as a third of the popular Democratic vote. In 1968, hoping to throw the election into the House of Representatives, where he could attempt to cut deals with supporters of the two major party candidates, Wallace ran again, this time as a candidate of the American Independent Party. Despite the inherent difficulty in running as a third-party candidate, Wallace carried five states, won 13 percent of the popular vote, and received an astonishing forty-six Electoral College votes. In 1972, he ran again and this time won Democratic primaries in Maryland, Michigan, North Carolina, Tennessee, and Florida (where he won more than 40 percent of the vote in a multicandidate primary). Wallace's campaign ended when he was shot during a campaign speech at a shopping center in Laurel, Maryland, and was relegated for the rest of his life to a wheelchair.

In Wallace, many southerners had found a true champion; now, with a national Democratic Party that was firmly committed not only to an activist and growing government but also to using the power of the federal government to end segregation and reshape the South, many of Wallace's supporters transferred their allegiance to the Republican Party. Wallace had often argued that there was "not a dime's worth of difference" between the Republican and Democratic parties; he and his supporters had decided to create that difference and, having failed to change the Democratic Party and having been unsuccessful at achieving power with a third party, they took aim at the GOP, which was virtually nonexistent in the South and ripe for an easy takeover.

Historically, Republicans had been far more resistant to big government than had the Democrats, who, since the beginning of Franklin Roosevelt's presidency, had aggressively used federal power to address a long list of economic and social concerns. Almost by default, the Republican Party had thus become the natural home for the conservatives who had propelled Goldwater's political rise. Now, however, just eight years after Goldwater conservatives had seized control of the Republican Party, they had serious competition in defining what the party would stand for.

Under the new southern influence, the party to which conservatives had tied their fortunes took on a very different shape, deeply (and narrowly) religious and comfortable with activist government (many wanted less federal involvement in racial matters and more in almost everything else). It was a far cry from the pro-liberty, constrained government philosophy Goldwater's supporters had championed. Now Wallace-ites and Goldwater activists found themselves in the same political party, attending the same precinct meetings and party conventions, and often backing the same candidates (at least in general elections). Slowly, the lines between these two originally distinct forces began to blur.

Fearful of further liberal control of the White House after the eight years of the Kennedy and Johnson presidencies, conservatives supported Richard Nixon in both 1968 and 1972, not out of conviction or admiration but simply out of a desire to nominate a candidate they believed could win. After Goldwater's lopsided defeat in 1964, there was no stomach for cries of "wait till next year"; instead, embarrassed promoters of the Goldwater candidacy joined with party pragmatists who could now cow conservatives into going along with a "winner" in exchange for a mere whisper of a hope that he would turn out okay. Thanks to his efforts to elect Goldwater and his subsequent election as governor of California, Ronald Reagan had become the new conservative hero, but Nixon was all but uncontested for the 1968 nomination.

Though conservatives had never thought of Nixon as one of them (he was, they believed, the ultimate pragmatist, unburdened by anything even faintly resembling belief or principle), the general public and the press nonetheless considered Nixon a conservative, and his forced resignation was yet another humiliation for conservative activists. By 1976, however, the conservatives who had originally rallied behind Goldwater were ready to again claim party control and were sufficiently strong that their candidate, Ronald Reagan, nearly succeeded in taking the party's nomination from a sitting president. Gerald Ford went on to lose the presidency, and four years later Reagan, who had launched his own political career in 1964 with a stirring nationally televised speech on Goldwater's behalf, was elected president. For Goldwater supporters, Reagan's victory was both a triumph and a vindication. Now, conservatism, centered on a strong national defense, reduced regulation, lower taxes, less federal spending, and more emphasis on individual freedoms, had won the White House. It was a heady moment.

In many ways, the Reagan era was a matured version of Goldwater conservatism. Reagan's principal domestic focus was on reducing taxes and replacing coercive regulatory practices with inducements for voluntary compliance. At conservative rallies, Reagan invoked the now standard denunciations of social hedonism, much as Goldwater had, but gave social-issue conservatives little more than lip service. He pushed aggressively for a stronger military with which to counter the Soviet Union, along the same lines Goldwater had advocated, in the belief that an enlarged military capacity would ensure peace, and in foreign policy he championed the cause of political liberty. Even as he strengthened America's armed forces and attempted to block the Soviets from securing toeholds that could endanger U.S. interests (generally by supplying indigenous forces rather than sending Americans into combat), his main weapons were rhetoric and negotiation, which he used to push for a reduction in the two nations' stockpiles of nuclear weapons.

But even as conservatives had emerged triumphant, and Ronald Reagan was at long last putting many long-standing and fundamental conservative principles into practice, the conservative movement was itself undergoing a transformation, and, like the metamorphosis about which Kafka had fantasized, the results often did not look good in the mirror.

New faces of "conservatism" sprang up. Some were merely extensions of the American-style conservatism of the Goldwater era, but others, such as the National Conservative Political Action Committee (NCPAC), feasted on emotional direct-mail fundraising appeals and focused on social-issue campaigns—guns, gays, flag burners, abortion, feminism.

Most compatible with the Goldwater ideal was the "New Right," represented most prominently by the charismatic New York congressman and former professional football star Jack Kemp, who was later to become a cabinet secretary and, in 1996, the Republican vice-presidential nominee. The New Right was primarily focused on a buoyantly optimistic economics and on the belief that, as John F. Kennedy had once observed, "a rising tide lifts all boats." Goldwater believed strongly in the power—and the morality—of free enterprise. This is what motivated Kemp as well, though he placed greater emphasis on expanding economic opportunity to a broader circle. The goal was a '60s-like focus on "power to the people," using the power of the free market to tackle poverty head-on. For years after leaving Congress and serving as secretary of Housing and Urban Development under the first President Bush, Kemp continued to push for broadening the Republican base and reaching out to minorities and the economically disadvantaged. During the 2007 debates over whether to allow the District of Columbia a full voting seat in the U.S. House of Representatives, a measure the current President Bush had repeatedly vowed to veto, Kemp was nearly apoplectic over the administration's position. "Young men and women are being sent from D.C. to Baghdad," Kemp told the *Washington Post*. "The hypocrisy is painful. It's just unbelievable how Republicans could turn away from American citizens who want to vote. I don't see how they can sleep at night."

The New Right represented a considerable departure from traditional Republicanism. Partly the differences were philosophical. The New Right had a strong Goldwater-style coloration—part traditional Republican, part libertarian, part populist—but it was also significantly different at a social level. New Right leaders included the children of poor Jewish immigrants, the son of a school janitor, and the grandson of steel mill workers. The term "New Right" was later incorrectly applied by some in the media to "social agenda" conservatives, but New Right conservatives were far more interested in working-class America—blue-collar workers, union members, blacks, small businessmen, and farmers—than in either the Fortune 500 or the enforcers of social propriety. To those in the New Right, it seemed unbelievable that American assembly line workers, carpenters, coal miners, and common laborers were somehow off-limits to Republicans. I had grown up wearing caps with AFL-CIO buttons on them, and I was elected to Congress, as a conservative Republican, with considerable support from both minorities and members of the so-called working class.

In many ways, the New Right shared the values of old-line conservatives: a belief in profit as the best incentive to production and as a creator of jobs, in limited government, in a strong national defense, in maximum individual freedom, in lower taxes and less regulation. But to those in the New Right, these things represented the philosophy of middle-class and working-class America. Whereas earlier fiscal conservatives strongly resisted increased federal debt, even short-term, these new "opportunity" conservatives contended that tax cuts—leaving more money in the hands of taxpayers—would not only be consistent with limited government and greater individual choice, but would also, by encouraging investment, result in economic growth that would produce more tax revenue than before. The primary emphasis was on reducing the "marginal" tax rates, which automatically moved citizens into higher tax brackets if they increased their earnings and thus served as a disincentive to productivity as well as to spending and investment.

As a part of this attempt to broaden the scope of conservative politics and to deal with the inherent problems associated with an economic underclass by expanding economic opportunity, New Right activists set out to persuade voters who had long opposed the policies of traditional Republicans that, in fact, the GOP was a more natural home for them than was the Democratic Party, which had moved further and further to the left. They made serious efforts to bring blacks into the fold, and new organizations of black conservatives sprang up. One group of New Right conservatives, of whom I was one, made a trip to the heart of labor union territory—Youngstown, Ohio, where steel plants had been shut down and unemployment was high—to urge local unionists to join the cause.

At first, a number of union activists were willing to listen and met privately with conservatives in a Youngstown motel. Their criticisms of government, and the Carter administration in particular, were as harsh as anything one might hear in the most Republican circles. Government spending, and the subsequent necessary government borrowing, they complained, had dried up the available capital, and the steel mills which had employed so much of Youngstown's labor force could not get the money to modernize, which they needed to remain competitive. They complained that the administration was failing to enforce antidumping laws, which would have imposed tariffs on imported products subsidized by foreign governments and sold in the United States at artificially low prices. Finally, they complained that the Occupational Safety and Health Administration and Environmental Protection Agency were burying steel manufacturers—their employers—under a flood of regulations that drove up production costs. We had found that these front-line labor union members were even more concerned about government excess than we were. But when word about the meeting got out publicly, higher-ranking labor leaders stepped in, and the effort quickly dissipated.

Had Jack Kemp run for president in 1996 with a focus on serious conservative issues—tax rates, low savings rates, international trade, national defense, expanding opportunity, bringing minorities into the nation's economic mainstream—the upbeat conservatism of Ronald Reagan might have received new life. But Kemp's advisors told him that in order to compete with a full Republican field—Bob Dole, Steve Forbes, Lamar Alexander, Phil Gramm, Richard Lugar, Pat Buchanan—he would have to devote a full year to fundraising. The prospect of a year on the road with his hand out was unappealing to Kemp. He stepped aside and later, when Dole selected him as his vice presidential running mate, Kemp was hamstrung by having to sing from the Dole song sheet, which was far too constricting. The moment had passed.

Nothing essential about the New Right agenda was incompatible with the Goldwater legacy, but some of its proponents were eager to pursue additional avenues as well. From the end of World War II to 1994, Republicans controlled Congress for only four years, from 1946 to 1948 and again from 1954 to 1956, despite years of very popular Republican presidents such as Dwight Eisenhower and, until Watergate overtook his presidency, Richard Nixon. This liberal chokehold on the lawmaking part of government was a constant puzzle to many conservatives, and thinking about that problem led to a seemingly simple answer. Nixon had repeatedly pointed to what he called a "silent majority," Americans who disapproved of the changed public mores that came to the fore in the turbulent 1960s but who were not engaged as fervently in the public arena as the young protesters of that era. The issue, it seemed, was how to end the silent majority's silence in terms of congressional representation. Many of the voters who supported Democrats had not made the connection between the votes they cast and a Congress that pursued policies that seemed, to many, to be insufficiently attentive to security threats, more concerned about criminals' rights than victims' rights, more protective of spotted owls than humans. Therefore, went the reasoning, what was necessary was to have somebody show voters how it was that their votes were being miscast. Because a great many of these conservative voters attended religious services regularly, the best place to reach them, it was thought, was at their place of worship, and the best people to persuade them were their own pastors, priests, ministers, or rabbis.

Although a number of conservative Christian organizations became involved in that effort, including Campus Crusade for Christ and the Christian Roundtable, the enterprise was not limited to any single religious perspective. Richard Viguerie, a conservative direct-mail entrepreneur, hosted a meeting in the living room of his home in McLean, Virginia, at which a religiously eclectic group of activists—Catholic, Protestant, Jewish, Greek Orthodox—discussed ways to carry a conservative political message to voters through their congregations. What was emerging from this and similar meetings was a new political force—the so-called Religious Right—that injected into the Republican Party a new emphasis on the promotion of religious morality (an area of concern which most early Goldwater activists thought belonged in the private, not public, and not political, arena). The focus of this new religion-centered "conservatism" was not on liberty and limited government but on what Russell Kirk had called the "transcendent moral order."

By 1989, the Moral Majority, the late Jerry Falwell's organization, which had emphasized religious values across sectarian lines and often shared a common purpose with many conservative and orthodox Jews, had all but disappeared. In its place rose the Christian Coalition, led by Pat Robertson and Ralph Reed. The Religious Right had become the overtly Christian Right.

Like George Wallace's supporters, the Christian Coalition's activists believed that the Republican Party, with its traditionalist predispositions, was ripe for a takeover. Here was a party that seemed to believe in many of the basic Christian values, but was not inclined to use politics or state power as a means to impose religious mores on a constitutionally secular nation. That could be changed.

In his novel *It Can't Happen Here*, Sinclair Lewis describes the rise of a fundamentalist political force bent on assuming national power. The principal protagonist in Lewis's novel is a charismatic preacher who succeeds in getting himself elected president. In the real-world politics of the '80s, the protagonist was a preacher named Pat Robertson. Robertson was the son of a U.S. senator (a Democrat from Virginia), and his goals were overtly political (Robertson himself ran for president in 1988). Through aggressive grassroots activism, the movement's members and supporters won elections, took over party organizations, and dominated party conventions. Later, when George W. Bush's political advisor Karl Rove would speak of "the "Republican base," this was who he had in mind.

The Christian Right was hardly the Republican base (the party's voters were often much more moderate in their views than were Robertson and his followers), but because Robertson's forces tended to dominate conventions and primaries, in which voter turnout is often low, they exerted influence far beyond their numbers. In the process, they transformed the Republican Party and indeed the conservative movement itself into an arm of religion, precisely the outcome the First Amendment to the Constitution was designed to prevent. They were instrumental in galvanizing conservative opposition to death with dignity laws in Oregon, private medical decisions in Florida, and scientific advances in the nation's medical laboratories.

How far this infusion of religious fundamentalism and social conservatism has skewed the public perception of political conservatism became strikingly apparent in two unrelated articles that appeared in the Saturday *New York Times* on May 5, 2007. One, on the newspaper's front page, carried this headline: "A Split Emerges as Conservatives Discuss Darwin." Darwin! According to the article's lead paragraph, "A dispute has cropped up within conservative circles, not over science, but over political ideology: Does Darwinian theory undermine conservative notions of religion and morality or does it actually support conservative philosophy?" The article went on to point out that during a debate, ten Republican presidential aspirants were asked whether they believed in evolution (can one imagine the Democratic candidates being asked the same question?). Three—Senator Sam Brownback of Kansas, former Arkansas Governor Mike Huckabee, and U.S. Representative Tom Tancredo of Colorado—said no.

My first reaction was that the article was a fake designed to make conservatives look silly (would the next article suggest that conservatives were divided as to whether the earth revolved around the sun?). But the story was real: Darwinian theory had been the basis of a panel discussion at the American Enterprise Institute, a respected conservative-leaning think tank. A full panel, including well-known conservatives George Gilder and Steven Hayward, had anchored a long discussion about bioethics, traditional morality, gender roles, sex education, euthanasia, stem cell research, global warming, and the extent to which the free market and the constitutional system of checks and balances rested on a platform of species evolution or biblical creationist tenets. This had been an actual conference, though how it related to "conservatism," a political philosophy of limited government, decentralization, political liberty, and a look-before-you-leap caution, seemed unimaginable.

Inside the paper, however, was another article recapping the presidential debate. "At G.O.P. Debate, Candidates Played to Conservatives: Views on Abortion and Evolution Vary." The lengthy article dealt with abortion, creationism, gay rights, and "how to balance their religious and secular values." This, then, had become the focus of how the press, the debate moderators, and perhaps even the public, saw "conservatives" and what was important to them. If this was "playing to conservatives" as the article's headline suggested, it was to conservatives who had nothing at all in common with the Constitution-centered activists who had created the modern conservative political movement.

The article quoted Whit Ayres, a Republican political consultant, as saying that although Rudolph Giuliani had appeared to hedge on the abortion issue (not really: he said that although he personally opposed abortion, he would understand if the Supreme Court, relying on judicial precedent, chose not to overturn *Roe v. Wade*), that might not prevent Giuliani from winning Republican primaries because the party's voters may consider other issues as more pressing. Ayres also suggested that having early primaries in populous states such as California and Florida would reduce the influence of "conservative voters" in smaller states, including Iowa. What Ayres was saying is that the actual conservative Republican base was not what so many self-proclaimed "conservative" spokesmen seemed to think it was.

The issue here is not religion or religious belief. An *ABC News* poll in February 2004 indicated that an overwhelming majority of Americans agreed with Brownback, Huckabee, and Tancredo. In that poll, 61 percent of respondents said they believed the Genesis story of world creation was quite literally true, and only 30 percent disagreed. And a *Time-SRBI* poll in October 2006 reported that a plurality (49 percent of respondents, compared with 41 percent) thought one could not simultaneously believe in divine creation and evolution. Biblical literalism is the American mainstream perspective. The issue is not religious belief but the degree to which it shapes public policy in a multicultural, multireligious society with a Constitution that protects minorities against the combined weight of the majority. That such a question must be raised, and seriously considered, reflects the enormous change wrought by the movement of the religiously conservative into the world of politics and their influence in shaping today's conservatism. At its founding in 1973, the Heritage Foundation described its mission as the formulation and promotion of policies based on four central conservative principles: free enterprise, limited government, individual freedom, and a strong national defense. Twenty years later, one more principle—"traditional American values"—was added to the list. Neither the mission statement of the American Conservative Union, adopted in 1964, nor the Sharon Statement, the declaration of principles of the conservative Young Americans for Freedom, refers to traditional or "social" values; like the original mission statement of the Heritage Foundation, they emphasize the Constitution, individual freedom, and free enterprise.

Even as religious fundamentalists were transforming conservatism, other forces were busy reshaping it as well. Conservatives had not only become the dominant voice of the Republican Party, but a majority of voters, or at least those who identified themselves with a political perspective, called themselves conservatives. (Liberalism had become "the L word," a label to be assiduously avoided by ambitious politicians; even in 2007, after Republicans had suffered the loss of both houses of Congress, and President George W. Bush was nearing all-time lows in presidential popularity, most voters described themselves as conservative.) It was therefore within conservative circles, and within the Republican Party, that anyone who shared at least some of the conservative movement's concerns could most effectively wield influence.

*Neo*conservatism clearly illustrates how much the "American," or Constitution-based, conservatism of the Goldwater era has been supplanted. Neoconservatives, for the most part, were traditional big-government Democratic liberals. Concentrated power in the hands of government officeholders didn't concern them (in fact, concentrated power seemed a necessity for ensuring that their ideas were implemented). Their affinity with conservatives lay in their opposition to the New Left counterculture of the '60s and '70s and what they perceived to be American weakness and vacillation in dealing with the persistent threat posed by the Soviet Union and its surrogates throughout the world.

During his campaign for the presidency, Ronald Reagan, who had committed himself to confronting Soviet military power, became acquainted with the writings of an Oklahoma-born Georgetown professor named Jeane Kirkpatrick. Kirkpatrick, a lifelong liberal Democrat and a former member of the Young People's Socialist League, decried what she saw as her party's abandonment of the hard-line anticommunism policies earlier championed by such liberals as President Harry Truman, Senator Henry Jackson, and Vice President Hubert Humphrey, for whom she had served as a campaign advisor when he ran for president in 1968. Reagan brought Kirkpatrick into his inner circle after reading her essay "Dictatorships and Double Standards" in *Commentary*, and after his election he named her the U.S. ambassador to the United Nations. In that position, she called attention to the pro-Soviet voting records of member nations that had been receiving generous financial support from the United States, and she urged Congress to link future foreign assistance funding to support for the American government's policies.

Kirkpatrick had continued to consider herself a Democrat even while working for Reagan and continued to push for more federal spending on liberal domestic priorities. In 1979, Kirkpatrick had written an article for *Commonsense*, a Republican magazine, titled "Why We Don't Become Republicans" (the answer: because Republicans did not spend enough on government programs). What Kirkpatrick was advocating was a firm stand against the Soviet Union and international communism, combined with a traditional liberal approach to solving social problems. But the Left wasn't buying it. The socialist Michael Harrington reportedly coined the term "neoconservative," which he intended to be derisive, arguing that Kirkpatrick and those who shared her views could no longer claim to be liberals. The term was soon used by neoconservatives to describe themselves. It became impossible for Kirkpatrick and her fellow neoconservatives to remain Democrats; they became full-fledged Republicans and a significant force within the party's policy circles, not at the grassroots level or in party conventions—these were increasingly the domains of the religious conservatives—but within the ranks of Republican administrations, often at the very highest of levels.

Kirkpatrick was joined by others, including Irving Kristol and his son, William, who was to serve as a top assistant to Vice President Dan Quayle and later to found the *Weekly Standard* magazine. All were strongly anticommunist and strongly antitotalitarian (Kirkpatrick, in *Dictatorships and Double Standards*, attempted to draw a distinction between "totalitarian" and "authoritarian" governments; she was opposed to both, but argued that the United States could justify continued support of authoritarian governments because they were more susceptible to eventual reform. The problem, of course, was that for the oppressed it mattered little whether their oppressors were described as totalitarian or merely authoritarian; they would hate their oppressors and the people who helped to keep their oppressors in power).

Disillusioned by the politics of such Democrats as George McGovern—Kirkpatrick called them the "Blame America First" crowd—and heartened by Reagan's election, neoconservatives had become the latest in a succession of non-Republican, nonconservative activists to move into conservative and Republican ranks. They continued to urge ever more forceful responses to perceived threats and reshaped the traditional conservative approach to national security. Neoconservatives brought into the conservative movement and the party a sense that the nation must act forcefully to counter any perceived or emerging threat, a significant shift from policies that had previously emphasized prudence. In the minds of most conservatives, the ultimate purpose of a strong national defense had been to deter war; now war was increasingly seen not as a last option, but as a useful tool for the nation to achieve worthy ends. Constitutional limits on the president's ability to wage war were considered almost quaint.

Activist Phyllis Schlafly, a member of the American Conservative Union's board of directors, once remarked that the conservative movement had come to depend on a coalition of disparate ideologies. Year after year, new forces pushed their way into the Republican Party and into conservative politics. By the time George W. Bush assumed the presidency, what had once been the focus of American conservatism—personal liberty and restrained government—had almost ceased to exist as a motivating force for the movement. Conservatives had finally attained power, but they had ceased to be conservatives, at least in the uniquely American sense of the word.

The changed character of the conservative movement may be seen most dramatically in the platforms adopted at Republican national conventions. Party platforms serve only a very limited purpose: other than a relatively small number of committed ideologues and partisan activists, very few voters actually have any idea what is in a political party's national platform, and most of the candidates who run for public office under a party's label tend to ignore the platform altogether. But the platforms do reflect the positions of the party activists who dominate the conventions. Here, in the platform, is what they believe the party and they themselves are all about.

Comparing the platforms of 1964 and 2004 is the political equivalent of comparing apples and oranges. Though the activists at both conventions used the same self-descriptive terminology, the political philosophies they represented were almost antithetical.

In 1964, individual freedom and decentralized power, as we've seen, were primary considerations. The fourth sentence of that year's national party platform, under the heading "For a Free People," reads, "Even in this Constitutional Republic, for two centuries the beacon of liberty the world over, individual freedom retreats under the mounting assault of expanding centralized power." A few paragraphs later, the platform stresses that "great power . . . must be so checked, balanced, and restrained and, where necessary, so dispersed as to prevent it from becoming a threat to freedom."

Four years later, with Goldwater conservatives now firmly in control of the Republican apparatus (though recognizing their inability to nominate one of their own, following the disastrous conclusion to Goldwater's presidential campaign), the theme of constraint—and separated powers—continued: "An entrenched, burgeoning bureaucracy has increasingly usurped powers unauthorized by Congress. Decentralization of power, as well as strict Congressional oversight . . . are urgently needed to preserve personal liberty."

Having observed President Lyndon Johnson's bullying of Congress, convention delegates insisted that "Congress itself must be reorganized and modernized in order to function efficiently as a coequal branch of government."

By 2004, there was no sign of concern about constraining centralized power or recognizing Congress as the presidency's constitutional equal. In fact, what had emerged came eerily close to being a "cult of personality." In 1964, the Republican platform was about freedom. In 2004, it was about George W. Bush. Conservatives now appeared quite comfortable with the idea of a strong, centralized government and a single powerful figure—a complete reversal.

All party platforms can be expected to make frequent and glowing references to "the president" or "the administration" when an incumbent president of that party is seeking re-election. One simple way to determine the extent to which principle has been supplanted by allegiance to an individual is to count the number of times that the incumbent president is praised by name within the document. These were, after all, supposed to be *party* platforms, put forth as expressions of what the party itself was all about, not hymns of praise to a leader.

Since 1964, there have been five elections in which an incumbent Republican president has sought election or reelection: 1972 (Richard M. Nixon); 1976 (Gerald R. Ford); 1984 (Ronald Reagan); 1992 (George H. W. Bush); and 2004 (George W. Bush). In 1972, when Richard Nixon was running against Senator George McGovern for a second term in the White House, the Republican platform referred to him by name twenty-eight times. In 1976, Ford's name did not appear in the Republican platform a single time despite the fact that he was now seeking the presidency in his own right (an omission that may have been at least partially ascribable to the heavy presence of Reagan supporters among the convention delegates).

Ronald Reagan, of course, was a far different story. Reagan's presidency was of vastly greater significance than Ford's, and Reagan was an outsized figure with a degree of personal popularity that quite often transcended party lines. As might have been expected, the 1984 Republican platform evoked his name seventy times. When George H. W. Bush ran for a second term of his own, his name appeared in the platform sixty-five times.

Then came George W. Bush. His father had generally been considered a moderate rather than a conservative, and he had been denied a speaking role at an annual Conservative Political Action Conference in Washington, D.C., even as Reagan's hand-picked vice president. But the son positioned himself altogether differently; he ran for president as a self-proclaimed "conservative," embracing the label enthusiastically. In fact, the younger Bush won the Republican nomination for president in 2000 largely by claiming that his opponents, including Arizona Senator John McCain, were not equally (and therefore not sufficiently) conservative. Observers often commented that Bush, then the governor of Texas, was politically more the son of Ronald Reagan than of his own father. He thus came to the presidency as the heir to the Goldwater-Reagan legacy. But whereas the Republican platforms of the past had concentrated more on principle than on a leader, the 2004 platform paid a distinctly personal homage to George W. Bush, citing him by name 228 separate times, sometimes four or five times in a single paragraph. This was *l'état c'est moi*, Texas-style.

While the "W" platform—a platform that amounts to little more than a hymn of praise to a party leader—is striking in its departure from previous party beliefs, there had been numerous other examples in recent years of a conservative willingness to invest ever-greater authority in the presidency. These included a persistent campaign to give presidents a line-item veto, essentially wiping out the founders' insistence that spending decisions should be made by the people's representatives, and the equally determined effort to establish congressional term limits, thereby weakening the institutional knowledge, skill, and effectiveness of the legislative branch. A party platform that was little more than a campaign brochure for an individual candidate was simply the next step along a continuum.

In 1964, when conservatives gathered at the Cow Palace in San Francisco to nominate a candidate and to challenge the existing political order, America was entering a period of profound social change. It was not yet the turbulent mid- or late '60s, but neither was it any longer the placid 1950s. Betty Friedan's *The Feminine Mystique* had become a national best-seller, and feminist politics— largely dormant since women had won the right to vote in 1920— was reemerging. In 1962, in *Engel v. Vitale*, the Supreme Court ruled that school prayer, a traditional first-class-period ritual in most of America's classrooms, was unconstitutional. Civil rights protests were spreading through the South and attracting sympathetic whites from other parts of the country. Though the Cold War continued, and Americans constructed backyard bomb shelters, a growing national peace movement sent marchers into the streets with "Ban the Bomb" signs and demands for disarmament. On college campuses, radical student organizations such as the Students for a Democratic Society (SDS) galvanized a more militant Left. The 1962

Port Huron Statement called for armies—and public education—to be placed under the jurisdiction of the United Nations.

One can only imagine what the 1964 Republican platform might have looked like had it been composed of today's conservatives. There would have been planks demanding the impeachment of Supreme Court justices; support for resolutions reaffirming the strong preference for the woman's "traditional" role as homemaker and supportive spouse; denunciation of participants in peace demonstrations for their role in undermining the morale of American servicemen and encouraging the expansionist military ambitions of atheistic Soviet communism; a demand for universities to crack down on the militant students they harbored.

But the 1964 convention was made up of men and women whose prime objective was to conserve the values of the American Constitution, not former Wallace-ites or members of the Christian Coalition or hawkish former liberals. Demands to impeach Supreme Court justices and evict the United Nations from its New York City offices were the domain of extremists in the John Birch Society. The central thrust of that year's platform was its emphasis on "liberty," "freedom," and constrained government. My copy of the 1964 platform runs twenty-three single-spaced pages; there was ample room to call for a host of constitutional changes or to issue denunciations or reaffirmations or to rail against the changing world if that had been the delegates' intent.

The Goldwater platform did not entirely ignore the social changes beginning to whirl about the delegates, nor did it shy away from calling for constitutional amendments as remedies, but by the standards of today, the response was notably restrained. It expressed a relatively mild complaint about "moral decline and drift" (sounding very much like the complaints coming from the student Left, with its emphasis on "the prevailing preoccupation with physical and material comforts") and contained some warm words for religious practice, blaming the "decline" on "indifference to national ideals rounded in devoutly held religious faith." The proposed solution? "Not to renounce this heritage of faith and high purpose, rather . . . to reaffirm and reapply it." The reaffirmation did not include a call for a collective or institutional response. This is what the 1964 platform said: "Every person has the right to govern himself, to fix his own goals, and to make his own way with a minimum of governmental interference."

Among the other things the platform contained were a call for new federal legislation to curb the use of the federal postal system for the mailing of "obscene" materials, and a constitutional amendment permitting the free exercise of religion in public places—provided that the religious exercises were neither prepared by, nor prescribed by, any government entity, including any local government, and were thus entirely voluntary. Rather than insisting, as many of today's conservative activists do, that there is no constitutional requirement for a separation of church and state, the 1964 platform described its proposal as "preserving the traditional separation of church and state." The entirety of this response to the Supreme Court's school prayer ruling was only four lines long and neither attacked nor called for the impeachment of any of the justices who issued the ruling.

The platform's reaction to civil rights demonstrations was mixed. It accused the Johnson administration of "encouraging disorderly and lawless elements" but also criticized the administration both for failing to fulfill promises to rights activists and for not helping the civil rights cause by enforcing existing federal laws more effectively. The platform called for the "full implementation and faithful execution of the Civil Rights Act of 1964 and all other civil rights statutes, to assure equal rights and opportunities guaranteed by the Constitution to every citizen." It called for improved civil rights statutes and for "additional administrative or legislative actions as may be required to end the denial . . . of the right to vote."

As for feminism, the Goldwater platform offered no precursor to the Rush Limbaugh–style assault on "Femi Nazis." In fact, the response was just the opposite. The 1964 Civil Rights Act, which the platform enthusiastically endorsed, contained a provision specifically prohibiting discrimination on the basis of gender (the work of Michigan Congresswoman Martha Griffiths). The Goldwater platform contained language laying the groundwork for explicit conservative support of an Equal Rights Amendment with its plank denouncing "discrimination based on race, creed, national origin or sex." It was the natural position for a conservative movement that centered on respect for individual rights, individual differences, and individual choices.

Had the delegates in San Francisco looked into a crystal ball and seen the federal government's formula for public education in 2008, they would almost certainly have stated, as did the delegates in 1964, strong resistance to "efforts which endanger local control of schools." It is unlikely, though, that they would have realized that they would be resisting the schemes of their fellow conservatives rather than the Democrats at whom they had aimed that attack. "Year after year freedom, diversity, and individual, local, and state responsibility have given way to regimentation, conformity, and subservience to central power," the 1964 platform complained. Reassemble those convention delegates today and one can imagine the same complaint being lodged, equally strongly, against the current administration and its enablers and supporters in Congress.

As I've noted, the conservative themes of the Goldwater years survived his defeat. Goldwater himself had temporarily left the political stage (he was reelected to the Senate in 1968, four years after his defeat for the presidency, and served for eighteen more years). But many of his supporters had built their campaign experiences into burgeoning political careers of their own, and they played a critical role in Republican Party politics for many more years. Their influence was felt again in 1968, at the convention that turned to Richard Nixon, considered the candidate most likely to be able to win and one with undeniably conservative credentials in the foreign policy arena, which continued to occupy center stage in American policymaking.

But foreign policy was not the only issue of concern by this point in the late '60s. Protest, assassination, war, riots, drugs, demonstrations, upheaval, sit-ins, lie-ins, die-ins: these were the social markers of the time. The Republican National Convention of 1968 was held in Miami, and though the disruptions were not of the same magnitude as those which famously roiled the Democratic convention in Chicago later that summer, Republican delegates traveling by bus to the convention could see police sharpshooters stationed on rooftops all along the route. American cities had become a domestic war zone. America's foreign policy, and the Vietnam War in particular, were key elements in the rise of the militant counterculture, but they were not the only elements. Racism, in all its forms, was still a major factor. Students taking over college campuses were protesting economic disparities as well as war casualties. Society was being challenged on many fronts. The American flag was being set ablaze or worn as decoration on the seat of one's tattered blue jeans. Conventional morality was ignored or ridiculed.

Now was the time, surely, to constitutionally prohibit desecration of the flag, to come down hard on the free love and free speech movements that were being used to undermine "the American way." Yet the 1968 platform declared that the Republican Party was "the only barricade against those who, through excessive government power, would overwhelm and destroy man's liberty." There is no mention of drugs. No mention of flag-burning. No denunciation of street protests. No calls for suppression of the long haired, pot-smoking, in-your-face younger generation. It was not that Republicans were not concerned by what they saw happening. But using the government to impose conformity or rewriting the national Constitution to achieve narrow social or political goals was simply not part of their lexicon. "We must give increasing attention to the views of the young and recognize their key role in our present as well as the future," the platform stated. "We must attack the root causes of poverty and eradicate racism, hatred and violence. . . . We pledge . . . concern for the unique problems of citizens disadvantaged in our total society by race, color, national origin, creed, or sex. . . . The Republican Party strongly advocates measures to alleviate and remove the frustrations that contribute to riots."

As for American youth, the instigators of the protests that were roiling the cities and college campuses, the platform said: "Our youth today are endowed with greater knowledge and maturity than any such generation of the past. Their political restlessness reflects their urgent hope to achieve a meaningful participation in public affairs. . . . In recognition of the abilities of these younger citizens, their desire to participate, and their service to the nation's defense, we believe that lower age groups should be accorded the right to vote." It was hardly a response one might expect of the "conservatives" of today.

The platforms of the years most closely following the 1964 conservative takeover of the Republican Party continued to call for passage of an Equal Rights Amendment and for giving the District of Columbia full voting representation in the U.S. House. Even in 1972, conservatives hammered away at their principal theme: individual liberty. "Every person is a sovereign being, possessed of dignity and inalienable rights," the platform declared. As part of that commitment, the platform vowed "to defend the citizen's right to privacy in our increasingly interdependent society" and to "oppose computerized national data banks and all other 'Big Brother' schemes which endanger individual rights."

Delegates in 1972 also called for increasing federal support for family planning. Again, consider the contrast with today's "conservatism." Barry Goldwater's wife was one of the founders of a Planned Parenthood chapter in Arizona, which annually gives a "Peggy Goldwater Award" to one of the chapter's leading volunteers and a "Barry Goldwater Award" to a legislator who has worked on behalf of reproductive rights. Yet in 2007, Republican presidential candidate Rudolph Giuliani was attacked by conservatives when it was learned that he had sent a small contribution to Planned Parenthood.

Clearly, support for women's rights would become one of the victims of the changed nature of American conservatism. Republican platforms had endorsed the Equal Rights Amendment since 1940, but in 1980, when Mary Crisp, the party's national cochairman, urged that year's convention to take a similar stand, she lost; for the first time in forty years, the party reversed its position. It again endorsed a constitutional amendment to ban abortion, as it had done for the first time in 1976. A strong Goldwater supporter, Crisp later asked, according to the *New York Times*, "How can we support freedom from government interference on economic issues but not on the most basic personal decision of all?" After George H. W. Bush's defeat for reelection in 1992, Rich Bond, the Republican national chairman during Bush's presidency, appealed to the party to end its opposition to abortion and "not cling to zealotry masquerading as principle." Crisp responded, "I wish he had made this speech before the election."

In *Fiddler on the Roof*, Tevye asks the village rabbi whether there is a blessing even for the czar. "Of course, my son," the rabbi replies: "May God bless and keep the czar—far away from us." That was the attitude that marked conservatism's perspective of government during the years of the Goldwater movement. It was not that no good was to be gained from government action (in fact, as noted earlier, the 1964 Republican convention urged aggressive action in defense of civil rights), but for the most part, citizens were to be left free to govern themselves, to set their own goals, to shape their own spirituality.

Gradually, however, as new forces moved into the party and declared themselves to be conservatives, things began to change. On the surface, the 2000 Republican platform still paid lip service to individual liberty ("Since the election of 1860, the Republican Party has had a special calling—to advance the founding principles of freedom and limited government and the dignity and worth of every individual") and civil rights ("Government . . . has a responsibility to protect personal privacy"). Beneath the libertarian veneer, however, was a new social vision couched in the rhetoric of "traditional" (that is, religious) mores.

Once again, the platform endorsed voluntary prayer, but without the earlier insistence on safeguards or any emphasis on personal liberty. Now there was a demand that religious groups be given access to public school facilities. The platform called for the government to work with "faith-based" organizations to deal with such social issues as "non-marital pregnancy." Whereas the 1972 platform had called for increased federal funding for family-planning programs, the 2000 platform called for such programs to be eliminated and replaced with "abstinence education" programs. And whereas earlier platforms had championed the right of individuals to make their own choices, the 2000 platform strongly opposed the right of those same individuals to receive information about abortion or, incredibly, even about contraception. Suddenly it was no longer clear whether public policy was to be shaped in keeping with the Constitution or the dictates of religious doctrine.

Whereas conservatives of the Goldwater years had been loath to turn the Constitution into a repository of policy prescriptions, by 2000 the platform was calling for one constitutional amendment to ban abortion and another to prohibit the burning of the American flag, even though it could be argued that the right of free expression was one of the great causes for which many American soldiers had given their lives. The 2000 platform also called for legislation to ensure that the Fourteenth Amendment's due process protections applied to the unborn and for the use of a litmus test to ensure the appointment only of those judges who would commit to uphold abortion restrictions rather than base their decisions solely on the specific issues before them (and the language of the Constitution). It also attempted to mandate the definition of marriage (traditionally a local matter), called for stripping courts of long-standing areas of jurisdiction, and attempted to prohibit gays from serving in the military. Barry Goldwater's famous observation that he didn't care whether soldiers were gay or straight so long as they could shoot straight was essentially dismissed as the remark of a senile old man who had lived in an alien age.

The 2000 platform was replete with references to "tradition," "abortion," "homosexuality," and "religion." Whether one agrees or disagrees with the substance of the positions taken, two things had become abundantly clear: first, that there seemed no limit to those matters upon which the convention delegates would not only pronounce judgment but demand government action; and, second, that religious conviction, more than the Constitution, would serve as the template for policymaking.

The 2004 platform recapitulated the "social" and "values" planks adopted four years previously. The platform touched upon every aspect of public and private life: abstinence, gays in the military, desecration of the flag, faith-based social guidance, families, abortion, school prayer, home schooling, and marriage. Again the platform called for stripping federal courts of their traditional areas of jurisdiction—denying citizens the right to go to court to determine whether federal mandates violated their constitutional rights. Gone were the old concerns about concentrated power and big government's ability to monitor our lives. What was touted was the creation of the Terrorist Threat Integration Center and "consolidating all U.S. government watch list information on suspected terrorists in the new Terrorist Screening Center." And the platform praised the US-VISIT system, which had been instituted to gather biometric data on all foreign travelers.

Perhaps nothing more strikingly illustrates the change than the attitude toward government spending. Earlier conservatives had routinely called for balanced budgets and fiscal responsibility. The 2004 platform sought to justify the escalating federal deficit. "It is important to view the size of the deficit in relation to the size of the nation's economy," the platform argued. Lyndon Johnson could not have said it better. There had been a reversal of priorities.

Conservatism now stood for government activism and bureaucratic reach. If Barry Goldwater initiated the conservative revolution, George W. Bush may have ended it. And nowhere is this clearer than in the slow and steady dismantling of the constitutional framework.

II

AND THE WALLS CAME TUMBLING DOWN

CONSERVATIVES AND THE
CONSTITUTIONAL FRAMEWORK

THE history of the United States began not with independence from Great Britain but with the ratification of the Constitution by the thirteen colonies. It was from the principles—and the unique structure—established in that remarkable document that the distinctive entity that became the United States came into being. It was an experiment in government unlike any that had gone before it, built on the self-rule of a people who were to be citizens, not subjects, led by officials, chosen by the people, whose delegated powers were to be carefully circumscribed. Like the most secure of houses, it was a structure that consisted of a foundation and roof and walls. Lots of walls.

The walls were built to do what walls do—to enclose some things and keep other things out. One such wall was erected between the presidency and Congress; presidents could not take the country into a war, but Congress couldn't try to manage the conduct of a war. Congress could establish the nation's priorities (by determining which programs and projects it would fund), but it could not manage the agencies of government. Presidents could agree to treaties with foreign governments, but the agreement had no effect unless Congress gave its assent. The president could select a nominee for the Supreme Court, but none could actually join the Court unless Congress gave its permission. Presidents could not authorize the creation of federal programs (that's Congress's job) or approve spending public funds for government programs. Both the executive and legislative branches were to be constrained, but Congress, as the most direct representative of the people, was in almost every regard (other than the management of war) to be less constrained than the president. The branches were distinct and deliberately separate, each retaining some significant checks on the other. Article I of the Constitution (the legislative branch) and Article II (the presidency) are brief and adjacent, but the wall between them is high and stout.

A wall was erected between the church and the state, too, as an extension of the founders' experience with religious persecution in Europe. Placing religion in a position to dictate, or heavily influence, national policy had led to sanctions, torture, murder, and war. European battlefields were littered with the corpses of men sent to war on behalf of one religious sect or another. In a nation founded on Lockean principles of individual rights, there would be no place given to sectarian terror.

The constitutional stand on the role of religion has been persistently misstated both by advocates of a church-based influence on public policy and by those secularists who become apoplectic over any public display of a belief in God. The reference to a purposeful separation between church and state, as many have pointed out, usually in an attempt to argue against the existence of such a separation, emerged from the personal correspondence of Thomas Jefferson, not from either the Constitution or the available materials describing the founders' debates over constitutional provisions. Nonetheless, it remains a clear expression of what Jefferson and the other founders intended in the First Amendment provision prohibiting Congress from establishing a state religion. But although religion was meant to be kept at arm's length in the public arena, religious believers were *not* required to remain outside government or to remain silent in public debates. Religious practice was neither encouraged nor constrained. The Constitution's so-called Establishment Clause quite clearly erects a wall with—as with all walls—two sides: there can be no official state religion, therefore no church can dictate to policymakers; and because there is no official state church, no church can take precedence over others, which means that churchgoers and nonchurchgoers are equally free to worship, or not worship, as individual conscience guides them. The wall protects minorities against a religious majority but it protects religious practice as well.

A wall was built as well between the lawmaking and administrative branches of government, which shared responsibility for directing the government's activities, on the one hand, and the judicial branch on the other. Though the Supreme Court is arguably the weakest of the arms of the federal government (it commands neither an army nor the federal purse), and its constitutional authority is limited, it has over time gained public acceptance of its legitimacy as the final arbiter of constitutionality.

The Constitution protects the legal process against political interference by either of the other two branches. Courts, after all, are about justice, not public opinion, and for America's Supreme Court, justice is measured by a law's adherence to the protections afforded by the Constitution. Thus the Constitution specifically guarantees that once appointed by a president and confirmed by the Senate, justices cannot be removed except under highly unusual circumstances; no president and no Congress can remove a justice merely because they disagree with his or her judicial findings. (The salary of a sitting justice cannot be denied or reduced, thus removing the ability of unhappy presidents or members of Congress to starve the Court into acquiescence.) Under the Constitution, no court can be frustrated in its search for justice by being denied the power to examine the case against an accused. The ancient right of habeas corpus—a requirement that an accused be permitted to have his or her detention justified, and a defense heard, in court—is explicitly guaranteed in the Constitution and cannot be set aside by either the president or Congress except in the event of an insurrection or a foreign invasion.

A wall was also erected between the federal government and those of the states and communities. The Bill of Rights, most notably in the Ninth and Tenth Amendments, makes explicit that all rights not specifically assigned to the federal government by the Constitution remain with the states or with the people themselves. In fact, central to conservative political thought is the belief that much of what properly belongs in the government sphere is more appropriately handled not by Washington but by local and state officials. "States' rights" ultimately became a pejorative term because racists hid behind it in an attempt to block the federal government from enforcing the constitutional rights of minorities within their communities, but while denial of civil rights was clearly not within the constitutional purview of local governments, other realms of authority did remain outside the federal bailiwick. Marriage laws, for example.

When Congress took up consideration of a proposed constitutional amendment to define the word "marriage," with all its social and legal ramifications, as referring exclusively to a relationship between one man and one woman, one of its most prominent members, Senator John McCain, appeared to take both sides of the issue. He was opposed to the amendment, but he favored an amendment to the Arizona Constitution prohibiting same-sex marriage. What McCain was doing was patching a wall. There are, constitutionally, two Americas. One is the "national" America, the one to which most of the Constitution applies by distributing elements of federal authority, setting limits on federal power, and so forth. The other is the nonfederal America, states and cities, each with its own realms of authority. Though constitutional protections apply to the states as well as to the federal government, many of the specific powers of governance were deliberately left outside the reach of the central authority. Defending the country against attack is a federal responsibility; traffic laws and marriage requirements fall to the states.

This does not, of course, mean that the federal government won't try to push the limits. For example, the Brady law—gun control legislation enacted by Congress in 1993 and signed into law by President Clinton—attempted to require local law enforcement officers to conduct background checks on people seeking to buy handguns. On June 27, 1997, in *Printz v. United States*, the Supreme Court ruled that the Constitution did not give Congress authority to assign such duties to local officials. Nine years later, the U.S. Court of Appeals for the District of Columbia stated the *Printz* finding this way: "The principle of the Tenth Amendment articulated in *Printz* is that the federal government may not direct, compel or commandeer state officials." The issue was not merely gun control, but the wall that the Constitution had erected between the federal and other governments.

Conservatives traditionally take the Ninth and Tenth Amendments literally, believing them to be as critical to the health of the nation as the better-known protections included in the First Amendment (freedom of speech, freedom of religion, freedom to assemble, freedom to petition one's government, and so forth). They are the cornerstones of the wall designed to buttress the limits on central authority. But there are practical reasons for the wall as well as philosophical reasons: although Idaho and Alabama are ill-suited to provide for the nation's defense, and Illinois and Nevada would be hard-pressed, on their own, to run a nationwide postal system, the national government is equally ill-suited to regulate the public schools in Massachusetts or Virginia (part of the reason for the strong conservative complaints about the Bush administration's "No Child Left Behind" program).

As the federal government has expanded, it has inevitably taken on roles it performs poorly. The one truly innovative element in the 1994 Republican Contract with America (to which I will return later) was its insistence on returning decision-making authority to the states and local communities. The answer in many cases is not for government to do nothing—there are legitimate roles for collective decision making and government action—but for the right government, the one closest to the people, to act.

Also inherent in the framework of the Constitution is a wall between elected leaders and the people themselves. The United States is not a pure democracy; it is a mediated, constrained, limited democracy. The majority, no matter how large, cannot shut down the scrutiny of the press, require a prescribed religious litany, reinstitute slavery, or prevent unpopular groups from expressing their opinions en masse or in direct lobbying of legislators. There are limits on the power of the leaders, limits on the power of the few, and limits on the power of the many. This is a nation of walls; when we talk of America as the freest nation on earth, what we're talking about is a freedom that depends on the existence of these walls. And the walls are beginning to crumble.

THE TRIUMPH OF FACTIONALISM

After the tragedies of September 11, 2001, in the midst of public apprehension about the nation's vulnerability to terrorist attacks, Bush administration officials waged an aggressive campaign to strengthen the ability of the president to make unilateral decisions about anything that could be even remotely connected to concerns about national security. In response to this effort to concentrate political power in the White House, a small band of lawyers, scholars, and journalists, concerned about the erosion of the constitutionally mandated separation of powers, joined together to protect what remained of congressional authority. These few die-hard "congressionalists" argued that they were less defenders of Congress as an institution than defenders of the constitutional framework that assigns those rights to Congress. It was a traditional conservative argument, but it was a defense of congressional authority in which Congress itself, during the years of conservative dominance, was often remarkably silent.

The level of congressional acquiescence was such that between the beginning of 2001 and the end of 2006, the Republican-dominated Congress often served merely as a rubber stamp for the White House. This is largely ascribable to conservative Republicans putting party solidarity ahead of constitutional responsibility. But there was also undoubtedly an element of ignorance.

A story will illustrate the point. During Reagan's presidency, a guerrilla force known as the Contras waged a civil war against the Sandinista government in Nicaragua. The Sandinistas were friendly with the Soviet Union and were building a new air strip, which Reagan's advisors feared might be used as a base for Soviet aircraft. The administration also argued that the Sandinistas were actively engaged in undermining several pro-U.S. governments in neighboring Central American countries. Reagan administration officials determined that it was important to American security interests for the United States to provide arms and money to help the Contra effort. And did so, with the help of a sizable number of Democrats, until a senior Massachusetts congressman named Edward Boland, a close friend and housemate of Speaker "Tip" O'Neill, managed to get the House to pass an amendment blocking further aid.

Later, I introduced, and persuaded the House to pass, an amendment supported by three of the leading Democrats in Congress (John Murtha, chairman of the Appropriations Committee's defense subcommittee; Claude Pepper, chairman of the House Rules Committee; and Dante Fascell, chairman of the House Foreign Affairs Committee) that authorized the United States to resume sending nonlethal assistance to the Nicaraguan rebels. But while the Boland amendment remained in force, the administration's supporters fumed. A member of my senior legislative staff urged me to give a speech on the House floor condemning what he considered to be an example of a blatantly unconstitutional congressional interference with the president's prerogatives. This (support for the Contras) is a matter of foreign policy, he said, and the president is in charge of foreign policy. I promised to give the speech if he would first enlarge a copy of the Constitution, put it on an easel, and highlight the sections that state that the president is in charge of foreign policy. When he returned, I asked if he had done what I asked. "I couldn't find it," he said.

Under the Constitution, *all* legislative authority is vested in Congress, not just authority over domestic law. Except for the fact that only presidents can negotiate (but not approve) treaties, and appoint (but not confirm) ambassadors, Congress is well within its rights—and well within its constitutional responsibilities and obligations—to take an active hand in shaping American foreign policy. For the later Republican Congress to have given President Bush a free hand in the foreign policy arena was not only a clear violation of the congressional oath of office but an appalling reversal of the conservative view that federal power should be limited, checked, and constrained. It was one thing to support a presidential initiative in foreign policy but something else altogether to insist that such decisions were his alone to make.

The premise behind the expansionist theory of the presidency is unsupportable both historically and constitutionally. The wall limiting presidential authority was erected not merely to enhance the prestige of Congress. Because both houses would have to agree to send troops to war, and spending and taxation bills would have to originate in the larger, popularly elected House (senators were originally appointed by state legislatures), the wall was intended to ensure that ultimate authority remained in the hands of the people. Congress does indeed have certain rights under the Constitution— clearly delineated areas of authority and assigned powers—but the role of Congress is less about power than about the legislature's obligations to the people.

There was a time when conservatives in Congress more clearly understood these obligations. When Reagan—one of this country's most popular presidents—was in the White House, conservatives opposed him on tax increases and major budget proposals. Many who bucked the president did so despite long-standing personal relationships with him and members of his administration.

On the night Reagan learned that he had lost the Iowa caucuses to George H. W. Bush, in 1980, putting his presidential hopes in jeopardy, I called him at his home in California and signed on to help in the campaign. I was named director of a campaign advisory team that included twenty different issues task forces, each co-chaired by a senator and a House member. I campaigned for Reagan in the snow and ice of New Hampshire, in the southern part of Florida—from Fort Lauderdale to Miami to the Keys—and on college campuses from southern Illinois to western Massachusetts. I was in a motel room in New Hampshire with Reagan and his wife, Nancy, when they received confirmation that he had won that state's important presidential primary. And yet I also opposed him on a major budget bill and—along with some seventy other conservative Republicans—on a tax bill. We admired Reagan, and most of the time we agreed with him. But it was our job—our constitutional obligation—to pursue the policies we thought best. The issue is not whether Reagan's proposals were better or worse than ours; what matters is that we understood, more so than many of today's conservatives seem to, that we were not part of the White House staff, that it was our obligation to reach an independent judgment on the issues, and that there were things more important than partisan solidarity.

Congress is America's *vox populi*, but too often in recent years, and more so when conservatives were in charge, that voice was disturbingly silent as Congress ignored its constitutional obligations. The branch of government responsible for regulating international commerce had created a new "fast track" approval process for trade agreements negotiated by the president, surrendering the right even to amend the treaties; under the new terms, legislators would have either to reject treaties in their entirety or accept them in their entirety, even when they included provisions counter to established public policy. Constitutionally authorized—and obligated—to set national spending priorities, Congress had even attempted to surrender control over spending decisions to the White House by granting the president an expanded veto power over individual congressional spending decisions, an abdication of legislative responsibility which was ultimately struck down as unconstitutional by the Supreme Court. Warned that a line-item veto, which would give the president de facto control over even the most minute spending decisions, would be a direct repudiation of the Constitution, conservatives decided to grant the president this new authority anyway, surrendering to the president their constitutional obligation to oversee national spending decisions.

Of all these, no single issue more clearly illustrates disregard for the Constitution than that decision to offer a president expanded veto powers. Doing so would allow the White House to unravel compromises that helped Congress craft a final legislative product important to fundamental national goals. During Bill Clinton's presidency, the conservative demand for a line-item veto grew so passionate that Speaker Newt Gingrich insisted that any final budget package include this unprecedented transfer of decision-making authority to the White House. Conservatives argued that the line-item veto was necessary for presidents to effectively exercise the veto power the Constitution had given them. This was an assertion based on the belief that the legislative practice of lumping together various spending bills unfairly tied a president's hands, forcing him to go along with spending that he opposed lest his opposition endanger more important appropriations. But it was an argument without basis: at the time Gingrich was demanding that Clinton undo the constitutional separation of powers, Clinton and his predecessors

Reagan and Bush Sr., had vetoed 136 bills, and Congress had over-ridden their vetoes only eleven times.

To understand the enormous scale of the power transfer, con-sider that a president needs the support of only one-third of one house of Congress to sustain a presidential veto. Imagine that Con-gress in 1996 (the year of Gingrich's demand) determined that the federal government should appropriate money for a project that legislators had determined to be in the national interest—rebuilding the protective seawalls around New Orleans, for example. Now imagine that bureaucrats working for the executive branch thought the spending unnecessary and prevailed upon the president to strike it out. Considered as part of a large spending bill, this single item might be protected from presidential second-guessing, but vetoed individually, Gingrich and his supporters argued, the item would have to stand on its own perceived merits during a congressional reconsideration.

One could argue that if the improvements to the seawalls were justified, Congress could simply reiterate its previous support. That, however, is a misleading argument that goes to the heart of why spending decisions, large and small, were left to Congress. Were the president given an individual-item veto authority, a power not granted by the founding fathers, the entire balance of power over spending decisions would be transferred from the people's repre-sentatives to the White House. In the case of the dispute over re-inforcing the seawalls in southern Louisiana, one could easily imag-ine a vote in which the House of Representatives overwhelmingly insisted on its original appropriation, perhaps by a vote of 435 to nothing. And the Senate, equally concerned about possible future hurricane damage to New Orleans, voted 66–34 to stand by its insistence on the improvements. What would happen? Despite op-position by 501 of the 535 members of Congress, because the bill's supporters did not win two-thirds of the vote in both houses, the president would prevail, the money would be struck from the appropriation, the new seawalls would not be built, and the people's voice would be silenced. That is the awesome extent of the unconstitutional power transfer that Gingrich and his fellow conservatives insisted upon.

How did such a dubious proposition gain such support? Of the eight Republican platforms adopted between the end of World War II and 1984, the only one mentioning the line-item veto (and only in passing) was during the 1972 convention, at a time when Nixon was so obsessed with presidential luminescence that he had ordered White House guards to dress in costumes that looked as though they belonged in a comic opera. Transferring spending authority to the chief executive was of a piece with the Nixonian notion of an "imperial" presidency but a far cry from anything conservatives had ever advocated.

What changed was that Reagan arrived in Washington determined to bring about fundamental change, much of it centered on a commitment to reduce federal spending. But Democrats continued to control both houses of Congress, which retained the power of the purse. As the Speaker, Tip O'Neill had a greater say over spending decisions than did the president. Neither Reagan nor the Republican Party had called for a line-item veto in 1980, when he was first elected, but he and his supporters in Congress gradually grew frustrated; they believed the people agreed with their program to cut spending, and they searched for ways to help the public understand that it was the Democrats, not Republicans, who were to blame for massive federal budgets. In effect, proposing a line-item veto was a public relations stunt to allow conservatives to tell voters, "Give us the power to reduce spending, and we will."

Edwin Meese, Reagan's attorney general, had reportedly advised the president in a private memorandum that the line-item veto was clearly beyond the scope of presidential power, in which case the sheer hypocrisy of the effort was even more shocking than the willingness to disregard the Constitution. Before the White House seized the issue as a political tool, the most prominent supporters of the line-item veto had been liberal Democrats. But for liberals, the line-item veto was fully consistent with their belief in empowering government to do what they considered necessary for the national good. Traditionally, conservatives had consistently shied away from making government more powerful. In 1964, the Republican platform called for "great power" to be "checked, balanced and restrained" and urged steps to protect the "power and prestige of Congress."

Before he demanded it in the 1996 "Contract with America" Gingrich himself had condemned the idea of a line-item veto. As so often happens, though, what began as a rhetorical device devised for its political effect began to take on a life of its own. Once conservatives had started making speeches and issuing press releases calling for a line-item veto, they could not subsequently back away. Reagan, and then George H. W. Bush, as well as congressional supporters, columnists, talk-show hosts, Republican Party spokesmen, and conservative activists institutionalized in local, state, and federal convention platforms this new call for a fundamental change in the constitutional structure.

On February 12, 1998, U.S. District Judge Thomas Hogan, appointed to the federal court by Reagan, reviewed the new law and found it unconstitutional. The law, he said, constituted an "unauthorized surrender to the president of an inherently legislative function." Accepting part of a bill and rejecting other parts is beyond the president's constitutional authority, the court declared. Four months later, on June 25, 1998, the Supreme Court, in an opinion supported by conservatives William Rehnquist and Clarence Thomas, upheld that decision, deeming the law unconstitutional.

But it didn't end there. In June 2006, President Bush gave a speech insisting that the White House be given a line-item veto. Senator Bill Frist, hand-picked by the president to serve as the Senate's Majority Leader (sufficient grounds for Senate Republicans to have chosen someone else), introduced new line-item veto legislation. This time, the surrender of power to the president would have gone even further: Congress would have only thirteen days to act on the president's proposals, would be denied the right to consider proposed spending deletions separately, and would not be permitted to offer amendments. Even if Congress overrode the president's vetoes, he could still refuse to spend appropriated funds for a period as long as six months, in some cases effectively killing the programs that Congress had mandated. As columnist George Will argued, the law would have provided the president with an unprecedented hammer with which to bludgeon members of Congress into doing as he wished. He could force them to back his proposals if they wished to avoid having him strike projects important to their constituents. Presidents, Will suggested, "would buy legislators' support on other large matters in exchange for not vetoing the legislators' favorite small items." What's more, Will said, the new veto power could actually result in more, not less, spending, further defeating the purported purpose of the proposal. "It is at least as likely that, knowing the president can veto line items, legislators might feel even freer to pack them into legislation, thereby earning constituents' gratitude for at least trying to deliver."

The story of the campaign for a line-item veto symbolizes the extent of the shift in conservative values. What once formed the core of conservative thought has been lost in the pursuit of other priorities, such as reduced spending and partisan advantage. It is difficult to know whether today's conservatives have consciously chosen to disregard the Constitution or whether questions of constitutionality simply don't intrude on their thinking, but this avid pursuit of unconstitutional goals is of a piece with the willing surrender of Congress's obligation to act as a check on presidential ambition. A Republican Congress, under conservative direction, virtually ceased any meaningful oversight over the executive branch even in the midst of a controversial and costly war. (By contrast, Democratic Senator Harry Truman, with the blessings of a Democratic Congress, conducted extensive hearings into the operations of the War Department during the presidency of another Demo-crat, Franklin D. Roosevelt.)

After regaining control of Congress in the 2006 elections, one of the first tasks Democrats had to face was restaffing congressional oversight committees that, as the *Washington Post* reported, "had all but atrophied during the six years that the GOP controlled Congress and the White House." (Ironically, the 1964 Republican platform, which had urged a more powerful legislative branch, had specifi-cally insisted on permitting the minority party "adequate staff.") Con-gressional oversight of the executive branch is not only one of the legislature's most important responsibilities, it is central to the con-servative goal of keeping government power within legal and con-stitutional limits. The Appropriations Committee provides the funds for all government programs and for the operation of all federal agencies and departments, including the White House. As a former member of that committee, I remember well its powers and its res-ponsibilities. I challenged questionable management of United Na-tions programs and persuaded the House to cut the level of American appropriations until reforms could be instituted; I challenged and blocked efforts by the Pentagon to understate the cost of Navy pro-grams and then shift money appropriated for other purposes to make up the difference.

But between 2001 and 2006, the investigations staff was, as the *Post* put it, "gutted." Staff members, apparently unaware that Con-gress had the authority to demand government documents, had taken to searching for them on Google or by filing information requests under the Freedom of Information Act. When Democrats regained control of Congress, the nonprofit and nonpartisan Project on Government Oversight began conducting workshops for leg-islative staffers to train them in oversight techniques. Iowa Senator Charles Grassley, a Republican who had been more willing than many of his conservative colleagues to question the Bush admin-istration, commented that it would be interesting to see whether the

Democrats "get results and make the executive branch work better for the American people or whether they just generate a series of embarrassing headlines for the White House." But of course if the headlines produced by the investigations are, indeed, embarrassing, that's all the more reason for the facts to come out.

There have been other failures to fulfill constitutional obligations as conservatives sought to be supportive of "their" president. To his credit, President Bush nominated two qualified jurists for seats on the Supreme Court. Although both John Roberts and Samuel Alito embraced judicial philosophies that many liberals would oppose, and most did, there was little doubt that both men possessed the intellect and the temperament to serve on the nation's highest court. But while the president did his job—he picked qualified nominees who reflected his views, as any president would have done—it was the responsibility of the Senate to question the nominees and gain assurance that they understood, and would be bound by, the Constitution and its limits.

For the most part, however, the confirmation process was pointless. Democrats pounded away at relatively minor and peripheral issues while Republicans asked the nominees questions not much more meaningful than if they had been asked to name their favorite Washington restaurants. The Alito hearings were the most egregious. Even as the Senate Judiciary Committee was considering Alito's nomination, the nation was caught up in an intense debate over the president's assertion that the Constitution provides him with the inherent authority to conduct wiretapping of American citizens without a court order, even though the law at that time clearly specified that only wiretaps conducted under a preapproved or retroactively granted warrant were legal. Yet not a single Republican member of the committee questioned Alito to any significant degree about his understanding of the constitutional separation of powers between the president and Congress, and the limitations on presidential authority. How could any senator, and especially a conservative, not want to know where Alito stood on such a fundamental question?

Indeed, as committee members were considering Alito's nomination, the administration's top mine-safety officials were defying a committee chairman's request that they remain at a Senate hearing to answer questions. The administration was busily engaged in trying to determine who had tipped off the public—and Congress—to the existence of secret overseas prisons, and the president was refusing to allow Congress to see documents about his administration's response to Hurricane Katrina or about the warnings that White House officials had received before the storm hit New Orleans and the Mississippi coast. Day after day, the president thumbed his nose at Congress, and, given the opportunity to question a prospective Justice of the Supreme Court about the boundaries of presidential authority, conservative senators sat mute.

What had happened was precisely what James Madison had warned against—the triumph of factionalism. "Solidarity" with one's party had become more important than the obligation of Congress to act as a body separate from, and completely equal to, the presidency. The separation of powers had taken a back seat to the quest for political domination, and Republican members of Congress increasingly looked like members of the White House staff.

The demise of deliberation has been buttressed by impatience with the constraints of the Constitution. The niceties of the t-crossers and i-dotters—those who concern themselves with whether a proposal is actually constitutionally permitted or at least marginally consistent with the requirements of good governance—are written off as nitpickers. To the true believer in party or ideology, constitutional limitations are the lace and snuffbox of politics: effete affectations that get in the way of the desired result.

This tendency has never been absent from American government, or perhaps from any government, but it is singularly disturbing to observe its prevalence within the ranks of conservative leaders. American conservatives long understood that there were people on the other side of the political divide who were more willing to push the limits of the existing legal framework to create that "better world" they so desired. Conservatives, on the other hand, had been the cautious ones, concerned about unintended consequences, examining and parsing proposed changes, arguing for "pilot" projects (small-scale tests rather than hopeful leaps). Conservatism was a "look before you leap" philosophy, insistent on checking out the landing area before jumping into something new. By 2006, however, it was a tendency long since abandoned. Conservatives had ceased to become the crossing guards cautioning citizens to look both ways; they had joined in the fun of visualizing a world that looked good to them and setting about to impose it on the nation. They had ceased to think, to reflect. And those who served in Congress were happy to set aside their own powers and cede them to the president if that would get them where they wanted to go.

The Speaker of the House during those six years when a Republican-dominated Congress coexisted with George W. Bush's presidency was himself a symbol of the problem. It would be hard to find anybody willing to say an unkind word about Dennis Hastert, the former high school teacher and wrestling coach who won the speakership after Newt Gingrich's resignation, but Hastert never grasped what it meant to be the leader of one of the three separate, independent, and equal branches of the government. A *Washington Post* article published just three weeks before the 2006 elections that ended Republican congressional dominance praised Hastert as somebody who had been "routinely underestimated," but the accomplishments that the article cited were unifying the party, expanding the size of the Republican congressional majority, and promoting President Bush's agenda. "He wakes up every morning thinking about how he can help the Republican team," one of Hastert's former aides told the *Post*. But Hastert had not been elected Republican leader (a job that went first to Tom DeLay of Texas and then to Roy Blunt of Missouri), nor had he had been named to head the party's congressional campaign committee. He was not a member of the president's staff. His job was to lead the branch of government charged with setting the national agenda.

Observers of Congress have long noted that the institution's various dysfunctions—restrictions on open debate and preventing consideration of minority viewpoints, for example—might lead to sufficient public dissatisfaction to gain support for greater centralization of power in the presidency, something the founders had struggled to prevent. It was assumed that the fear of such a result—strengthening the chief executive and undermining the people's legislature—would eventually lead Congress to reform its operations to regain the public trust. Few could have imagined that Congress was to fall into the hands of people who would actually prefer to surrender their authority—and their responsibilities—to the White House. In January 2006, when President Bush stood in the House chambers and delivered his annual State of the Union message, he once more urged Congress to give him the power of a line-item veto, and once more conservatives roared with approval. What had once been an attempt to strip power from Congress because it was controlled by Democrats had now become so much a part of the conservative litany that they cheered at having *their own* power taken away.

After forty years in the congressional wilderness, conservatives had finally won control of the House and Senate. Yet by the end of six years of the Bush presidency, the legislative branch had become just another executive branch agency, waiting for orders from the president and his staff. If the president had been guilty of malfeasance, as some of his critics have suggested, conservatives in Congress had been guilty of nonfeasance, an almost criminal failure to perform their public duties.

MADISON'S NIGHTMARE

If any single individual is primarily responsible for the "walls" constructed by the Constitution and therefore for giving shape to

American democracy, that individual is James Madison. What Thomas Jefferson was to the Declaration of Independence from Great Britain, Madison was to the document that established the nation's governmental structure, with its carefully designed system to keep the national government within reasonable bounds.

Knowing that this new nation would envelop a wide variety of economic and cultural interests—individual states that continued to maintain significant levels of sovereignty, an energetic and rapidly growing northern commercial and industrial class, a rural and largely agrarian South, pro-British and pro-French sentiment— Madison feared that powerful self-interested factions would cause the whole to splinter. To protect against this, he strongly resisted the development of political parties (organized factions which would each seek to dominate the government) and fashioned instead a system of competing interests *within* the government, giving each of its three branches very specific roles in the belief that the ambitions of each would keep a firm check on the ambitions of the others.

Shortly before the 2006 congressional elections, editors of the *Washington Monthly* magazine asked me to contribute an article to a pre-election edition in which prominent conservatives would argue that the nation's best interests would be served by returning control of Congress to the Democrats. The argument was based on the belief that the only way to effectively rein in the Bush administration was to return to divided government, with Congress in the hands of the "opposition" party. I had written articles and given speeches critical of the administration's apparent disdain for limits on presidential power, but I declined to contribute to the issue because I was disturbed by the underlying premise of the magazine's proposed solution. If the only way to curb a runaway presidency was to elect a Congress of a different political party, I realized, the Madisonian framework had failed and the intense partisanship Madison had so feared had come to full fruition.

The Constitution's separation of powers had been largely effective despite the fact that before Madison's death—before even his presidency—political parties had become a serious force in American politics. By the end of George W. Bush's sixth year in the White House, however, the wall of separation had disintegrated, primarily because the Republicans who dominated both houses of Congress had simply failed to do their job. The foxes were guarding the henhouse, and the nation was paying the price. The results were felt in many ways: failure to adequately question the administration's war plans, including manpower and equipment requirements and its postwar strategy for rebuilding Iraq; Americans having their phones illegally tapped and their personal financial records turned over to federal agents; expensive federal programs such as the Medicare prescription benefit enacted without a realistic understanding of the cost. Congress's abandonment of its constitutional responsibilities was felt in dollars wasted and, worse, in lives lost.

Part of the responsibility for this abandonment of legislative duty (and, simultaneously, the abandonment of the most basic fundamentals of American conservatism) can be traced to the emergence of a highly ambitious backbench congressman from Georgia: Newt Gingrich. Even before being elected to a party leadership position, Gingrich had aggressively pushed congressional Republicans in a new direction in which the pursuit of power trumped all other considerations. Gingrich cannot, of course, bear the full blame for what has happened to America's political system; for a number of reasons, "winning" has often replaced principle as the primary purpose of politics. But though Gingrich did not start the trend, he certainly hastened it along and took it to disastrous new levels.

Gingrich entered the House in January 1979, after having been defeated in two previous campaigns for Congress, and immediately began to climb up the political ladder. His ascent was carefully staged: a former teacher, Gingrich was careful to always let himself be seen clutching armloads of books, files, and papers as he strolled through congressional hallways; in meetings, he distributed lengthy bullet-point presentations, often stating the obvious but with fanfare. He organized conservatives, who had long been frustrated by

Democratic domination of the congressional agenda, into a cohesive group called the Conservative Opportunity Society. And he persuaded a more senior congressman, the late Guy Vander Jagt of Michigan—chairman of the National Republican Congressional Committee, the campaign arm of House Republicans—to turn over to him and his allies the task of mapping out a plan to drive Democrats from power.

Gingrich believed that the key to gaining power was to change the nature of congressional elections: from one-on-one races, decided by choices between individual candidates and the concerns of local constituents, to a nationwide referendum between warring political parties, much like the parliamentary system common in Great Britain and other democracies (a model the founders were familiar with and had chosen not to follow). To recruit new Republican candidates, Gingrich used not only the considerable resources of the campaign committee but took over a small grassroots Republican organization called GOPAC, established originally by former Delaware Governor Pete DuPont, and began an aggressive mass mail campaign to deliver "inspirational" messages and hard-hitting campaign advice—all in the form of taped speeches featuring Gingrich—to potential Republican candidates throughout the country. The goal was to get everyone singing the same political tune. Republican incumbents were subjected to intense pressure to take campaign money provided by their own supporters and put it into a common pool to be used to elect still more Republicans. To meet the common goal—and thus remain viable contenders for party leadership positions, participation being a prerequisite for consideration—Republicans set up new "leadership" political action committees and leaned heavily on Washington lobbyists for contributions.

The last obstacle in Gingrich's path to power was the popular House Republican leader Bob Michel of Illinois. A decorated war veteran who had served in the House of Representatives for nearly forty years and had gradually moved up the Republican leadership ladder, Michel had served as the party's whip, the number two leadership position, before succeeding John Rhodes of Arizona as the leader. He was firmly committed to the Republican Party's core beliefs and received high scores on "conservative" voting tabulations by the American Conservative Union, but he also believed that Congress should not merely offer a forum for partisan warfare but should deal legislatively with the nation's problems, which often meant finding areas of compromise with the Democrats who controlled the House. Gingrich determined to get rid of Michel; when the House Republican whip, Dick Cheney, was tapped by the first President Bush to become secretary of defense in 1989, Gingrich made his move, defeating Representative Ed Madigan of Illinois, Michel's choice for whip, by just two votes.

For the next five years, Michel continued to retain the title of Republican leader, but Gingrich exerted more and more control over Republican strategy and drove the party into an ever-more confrontational pattern of behavior, using one-minute speeches at the beginning of each legislative day and "special orders" (time set aside for general pronouncements at the end of legislative business)—normally occasions for pro forma rhetoric—to launch a barrage of partisan broadsides against Democrats. Effectively marginalized as the party's leader, Michel finally announced his retirement in 1994. From that point forward, partisan warfare was to be the new focus, almost the only focus, of congressional Republicans.

In the 1994 elections, Republican congressional incumbents were pressed to sign on to a single common document called a "Contract with America," essentially a rehash of various focus group-tested "reforms" designed to sharpen the distinction between the two political parties. Republicans were gathered together on the Capitol steps to show their allegiance to the "contract" and to display their unity.

One important part of the "Contract with America" was a pledge that if Republicans took control of Congress they would act to launch a constitutional amendment to set limits on how long a member of the House or Senate could serve. Given the public's natural inclination to be critical of officeholders—a cynicism that has often been well earned—it was a superficially attractive proposition. Fred Thompson, the former senator from Tennessee, had initially run for office in 1992 by campaigning against the very Congress he was seeking to join. "Cut their pay and send them home," Thompson cried, calling for term limits for the House and Senate, a reduction in congressional salaries, and the creation of a junior-partner-style national legislative body that would meet only half of each year.

Thompson was essentially calling for the creation of a new political system in which the role of the people's representatives would have been severely diminished (a direct repudiation of previous conservative calls for a more assertive Congress) and both the presidency and the federal bureaucracy would have been strengthened. The result would have been a reduced congressional ability to perform oversight, conduct hearings or investigations, or develop public policy (the constitutional roles specifically assigned to the legislative branch). In addition, Washington lobbyists would have had their hands strengthened as well, as a term-limited, part-time Congress became increasingly dependent on outside expertise as it struggled to deal with issues ranging from national defense to health care to agriculture to public transportation. Four years later, Thompson's ideas were adopted by his fellow Tennessean, former governor (and cabinet secretary) Lamar Alexander. Alexander ran for president with a campaign that attempted to appeal to populist sentiment by advocating both term limits and "a part-time citizen Congress." The campaign never got off the ground.

The term-limit campaign was predicated on an assumption that Congress is a never-changing body in which the same 535 men and women exercise political control for decades at a time. Set aside for a moment the argument that Congress was designed to be the equal of the executive branch (a literal reading of the Constitution would actually suggest that Congress, the "first branch," was to be the superior of the two branches), and that the "equality" envisioned by the Constitution would necessarily require a sufficient degree of experience and expertise within the legislature. Set aside the argument that in a democracy, the people should be entitled to choose whomever they wish to represent them in Washington—to toss out "representatives" who didn't adequately represent them or to re-elect over and over again those men and women whom they believed to be representing them, and their interests, well. Set aside even the strange notion that a low rate of turnover in Congress is proof that the system has failed and that the only way to demonstrate that a democracy is working is if the voters continually decide they have previously chosen unwisely and repeatedly toss out of office the representatives they have earlier selected, a political Catch-22 with only repeated failure serving as proof of success.

At the time conservatives were launching their campaign for term limits, there was already enough turnover to cause serious constitutionalists to worry that Congress would lack a sufficient number of experienced legislators to match the massive federal bureaucracy and the rapidly increasing number of presidential personnel (now somewhere between sixteen hundred and eighteen hundred, housed either in the White House or in the nearby Executive Office Buildings) in the ongoing debate over public policy decisions. In 1994, as congressional conservatives pushed for term limits, I reviewed what had been happening in my own home state of Oklahoma, which was then the latest state to decide that term limits were the only way to get rid of perpetual officeholders. On the very day the state's voters approved term limits, Democratic primary voters in Oklahoma's Second Congressional District defeated their incumbent House member, Mike Synar, which meant that the following January the state would be represented by a congressional delegation in which only one of its senators and none of its House members had been in office six years earlier, when George H. W. Bush had been elected president. The most senior member of the state delegation would have served in Congress for a mere four years.

In fact, in the fourteen years since Reagan's election in 1980, Oklahoma had had three governors, with a fourth to take office in a few months, and five Oklahomans in the state's two U.S. Senate seats. The First Congressional District would be on its third representative since the beginning of Reagan's *second* term; the Second District would be on its third representative since Reagan's initial election; the Third District was on its second in that time; the Fourth District was on its third; and the Fifth and Sixth Districts each on its second. Between January 1980 and January 1994, fifteen people held Oklahoma's six seats in the House. What's more, in 1980, five of the state's six House members were Democrats; after the 1994 elections, five of the six were Republicans. Without legislation weakening Congress's ability to serve as the constitutionally designed check on the White House, the state's voters had worked real change.

What, then, was the real reason behind the conservative love affair with this undemocratic proposition? The same as the reason behind the push for a line-item veto: it was a weapon in a partisan war. At the time conservatives wrote a promise of term limits into the "Contract with America," the House had been controlled continuously by Democrats for forty years. If voters could be convinced to toss out incumbents, Republicans might gain additional seats. Supposedly high-minded reform proposals were put forth as a ploy to gain partisan political advantage. But these proposals were in fact unconstitutional, since the Constitution itself sets out the qualifications for election to Congress, and Congress could not add as an additional prerequisite that one not have served previously. And that is precisely how the U.S. Supreme Court ruled in May 1995. Gradually, those states which had adopted term limits on their own legislators have reconsidered the wisdom of such a proposition even at the state level: as of 2007, either by court decision or otherwise,

Idaho, Massachusetts, Oregon, Utah, Wyoming, and Washington had dropped their own term-limit experiments.

There are mixed assessments as to how great a role the "Contract with America" and the nationalization of the 1994 elections played in wresting control from the Democrats (President Clinton had not covered himself with glory in his first two years in office), but from that point on, loyalty to party rather than to constituent (or even personal) preferences became the essential qualification for every aspirant to a Republican leadership position or committee chairmanship.

The Republican Party had always had its share of outliers, men or women who split from party ranks on occasion, either out of principle or to represent their constituents' views on a certain issue. For example, Silvio Conte of Massachusetts served as the senior (ranking) Republican member of the House Appropriations Committee. It is the job of the party whip to maximize the party's vote count on every issue to reach the House floor. Assistant whips would be positioned at every entrance to the chamber to remind fellow party members, as they entered, that the party vote was either "aye" or "nay," depending on the bill or amendment being considered. Often, however, a whip might say to Conte (or another Republican in similar circumstances): "We're voting 'yes' on this, but you probably want to vote 'no.'" It was a way to help more moderate members stay true to their principles and avoid getting into political difficulties with the voters back home. After the beginning of the Gingrich era, however, failure to vote along party lines was more likely to jeopardize anyone's chances of moving up within party ranks. Party loyalty, unity, and a common front against the political enemy constituted the new Republican system.

Over and over, Republicans under Gingrich's leadership forced the House to vote on "wedge" issues—proposals that had no chance of passage but were designed solely to force Democrats to cast votes that might make them more vulnerable to an election challenge.

During my years as national chairman of the American Conservative Union, we rated politicians by how they voted on important issues, not on whether those issues had originated in one political party or another, and we took the votes as they came: if dozens of Democrats had won high scores, we would have been delighted. But not any more. Instead of cheering happily and exchanging high-fives when Bill Clinton or a congressional Democrat offered a conservative proposal, Gingrich and his partisan warriors denounced Democrats for stealing their ideas.

The scorched-earth approach continued even after Republicans won control of Congress and should have transcended their besieged-minority mind-set and set about providing serious legislative direction. The result, eventually, was a public backlash, in which voters trimmed the party's vote margin in the House—a repudiation that led to Gingrich stepping down as Speaker and leaving Congress. Though no longer in the House, Gingrich continues to try to shape Republican strategy and behavior. After voters ended his party's control of Congress in November of 2006, House Republicans gathered at a Chesapeake Bay resort on Maryland's Eastern Shore to lick their wounds and ponder their future. Gingrich was there and again urged his fellow Republicans to "think outside the box," his favorite saying, even though it was precisely "thinking outside the box," breaking the mold of acceptable legislative behavior, that had finally done his party in. Asked about Gingrich's advice, the new Republican leader—now a leader of the legislative minority—John Boehner of Ohio responded, "It was just Newt being Newt. There was nothing new there."

In the early days of their post-Goldwater resurgence, conservatives were always quick to point out that they felt no particular loyalty to the Republican Party. They were conservatives first; the party was merely the best available vehicle for translating their beliefs into governing principles. After all, Reagan, Goldwater's successor as the nation's most prominent conservative, challenged an incumbent Republican president's nomination. And when President Reagan agreed to a tax increase, his conservative colleagues in Congress voted against him in large numbers. But Gingrich had transformed the process: instead of a tension between separate branches of government, as intended by the founders, it was now between political parties. Neither insistence on congressional prerogatives (and constitutional obligations) nor adherence to conservative principles mattered so much any more: what counted now was winning the battle for positions of authority, and if that meant weakening the Constitution and abandoning principle, so be it. When a Republican president was elected, this new fealty to party solidarity was reflected in an almost unquestioning loyalty to the White House. The two parties had trumped the three branches—and the results were a nightmare.

THE AMERICAN MONARCHY

On April 18, 2006, in response to a reporter's question about whether Donald Rumsfeld would be retained as the secretary of defense, President Bush replied, to the great delight of political commentators and standup comedians, "I'm the decider, and I decide what's best." It is almost beside the point that in that particular instance—the right to choose who would serve in his cabinet—Bush had it right; to the president's critics, and even to many of his friends, the comment seemed more revealing than Bush may have intended.

Many presidents have stretched the boundaries of their constitutional authority in times of crisis. As Arthur Schlesinger Jr., pointed out in *The Imperial Presidency,* Abraham Lincoln, in the midst of a civil war that threatened to destroy the union, "asserted the right to proclaim martial law behind the lines, to arrest people without warrant, to seize property, to suppress newspapers, to prevent the use of the post office for 'treasonable' correspondence, to emancipate slaves, to lay out a plan of reconstruction." Other presidents tried to expand their authority without the justification of a civil war, and they did so in a number of ways, including Richard Nixon's attempts to block the release of incriminating evidence by hiding behind claims of "executive privilege," a tactic that President Bush has found particularly attractive. Franklin Roosevelt attempted to pack the Supreme Court with justices favorable to his policies. Harry Truman tried to take over the steel mills. But when it comes to presidential overreaching, Bush is in a class of his own. No president in American history has conducted such a relentless, persistent campaign, on so many fronts and through so many means, to centralize political power in his own hands. A free society needs the truth to survive; protecting the public's capacity to know the truth is an imperative the nation cannot ignore. Yet the Bush administration, whether as part of its declared "war on terror" or its deliberate lying to Congress about the projected cost of a prescription drug benefit to be incorporated into the Medicare program, has been unrivaled in its penchant for keeping information from both the public and Congress. In August 2006, the *New York Times* reported that Pat Roberts, of Kansas, the Republican chairman of the Senate Intelligence Committee, "lashed out at the White House" for trying to keep secret from the public a part of the Senate's own internal report on the role played by Iraqi exiles in the administration's attempt to build support for the war against Iraq, a critical issue given assertions that the White House gave undue credibility to Iraqi citizens whose long absence from that country raised serious doubts about the reliability of their information.

In fact, defiance of Congress has been a hallmark of the Bush administration. Concerned about the theft of a laptop computer containing sensitive personal information about veterans, the House Veterans Affairs Committee had asked the Department of Veterans Affairs to report to Congress on the security of its information systems. In September 2007, *The Hill*, a Washington newspaper, reported the VA's response: "A secretly recorded meeting of researchers working for the Department of Veterans Affairs indicates that the department did not take seriously congressional requests intended to safeguard the personal and medical information of veterans." The newspaper reported that Dr. Joseph Francis, one of the administration's top VA officials told his research staff, "It's about power, it's about Congress saying, 'VA, you're accountable to us. We're not asking people to do an A-plus job on this report.'" The paper quoted the unidentified whistleblower who had secretly taped the meeting as saying, "When Congress does step forward to do something good, the agency takes it very casually and cavalierly." And, in fact, according to the article, Francis himself makes clear how the administration views congressional directives. "In 1996," he says on the tape, "legislation was passed . . . that really set the timing for all agencies to follow certain types of business principles in IT procurement and IT management, including cyber security. We've basically ignored that."

No president—in fact, not all of the previous forty-two presidents combined—has so aggressively or repeatedly declared the right to simply ignore laws that would restrict his power. This is, of course, a fundamental rejection of essential conservative principles, which Goldwater famously declared to be the maximizing of freedom. George Bush's operating principle seems to be the maximizing of federal, and especially executive, control.

President Bush's power grabs violate not only the most basic of conservative principles but also the central idea of American government that power should be divided and that important policies be subject to the scrutiny and deliberation inherent in the tension between competing centers of authority and responsibility. In the years of his presidency, the United States has illegally tapped the phones of American citizens, held prisoners for indefinite periods without trial or charges, and ignored treaty obligations. In each case, the president had the option of pursuing the same course legally—asking Congress to revise existing law to allow him to do what he believed necessary. But like his father, who only very reluctantly agreed to a congressional vote to authorize military force in the first Gulf War (after repeated insistence by Republican congressional leaders, myself among them), the son was highly reluctant to lend credibility to the suggestion that he needed permission to do what he thought best. He was, after all, "the decider."

Proclaiming his determination to use every weapon at his disposal to handle terrorist threats, the president at one point launched an ambitious cross-country speaking tour to persuade a skeptical public that the task of keeping the nation safe justified authorizing federal agents to eavesdrop on overseas telephone calls made by American citizens. The president's argument was merely a version of the old shell game, in which members of the audience try to follow the path of a dried pea hidden under a walnut shell as the shells are rapidly shuttled back and forth, in and out, to and fro. The misdirection leads the viewer to lose the pea. The real issue was not electronic surveillance at all. The issue was, Who decides? Despite his claims to being the nation's decider-in-chief, the president did not have the authority to make that decision. Congress decides, and if it is decided that the requirement of a court-ordered warrant is in need of revision, it is up to Congress, not the president, to make that change.

The president has also resisted efforts by Congress to elicit testimony from White House operatives. Previous presidents, Democrats and Republicans alike, have permitted their assistants to testify before Congress and had done so going back to George Washington's time. President Bush's deputy press secretary, Dana Perino, announced the administration's willingness to send White House officials to be "interviewed" by some members of Congress (as opposed to testifying in public hearings). However, she also explained why Congress should not try to compel testimony by issuing subpoenas: "We don't have any responsibility to you, and you don't have any specific oversight over the White House." Her response prompted Bill Clinton's former chief of staff, John

Podesta, to write in the *Washington Post* that thirty-one of Clinton's senior aides, including himself, had testified under oath on fifty-one separate occasions.

As I've emphasized, the entire framework of American government consists of walls specifically designed to prevent an elected and nonhereditary, but nonetheless powerful, American monarchy. Over the years, politicians have rebelled against the constraints imposed by the Constitution, whether it was Thomas Jefferson, eager to conclude a deal to purchase the Louisiana territories before the French changed their minds; antigun activists frustrated by the Second Amendment guarantee of the citizen's right to keep and bear arms; or advocates of a line-item veto. Left and Right, many have sought ways to change, circumvent, or ignore the Constitution. What is most startling about President Bush's overreaching is the scope and persistence of his disregard for the Constitution and the fact that it is being pursued by a man who calls himself a conservative even as he pursues policies that the founders of modern conservatism would have found both appalling and outrageous.

Ad hominem attacks on Bush's intellect or honesty or psychological motivations—a presumed rivalry with his father, for example—cloud the real issue. What is frightening is to have a president who lacks an understanding of, or is dismissive of, constitutional constraints on his authority. The Bush presidency has been marked by an arrogance of power. It has also been marked, as many have observed, by an unusually high degree of incompetence, at least partially ascribable to the president's tendency to award important positions to people whose primary qualification for these new responsibilities is a personal loyalty to the president. But incompetence the nation can survive. It can even survive involvement in an unwise war. What it cannot survive without lasting damage is a presidency that arrogates power unto itself, shuts down the deliberative process, ignores the law, and unilaterally assumes the regal trappings of a national "decider-in-chief." If Bush is, indeed, as Princeton historian Sean Wilentz suggests, the worst president in American history, it is not because of specific decisions he has made but because he has rejected the fundamental principles of American government.

Advocates of expanded presidential authority argue that a framework established in a time of sailing ships and muskets is inadequate to a time of weapons of mass destruction. And even in the absence of direct military threat from abroad, they argue, the size and scope of modern government requires a level of efficiency possible only under the direction of a centralized authority. (The "unitary executive" championed by President Bush would essentially end meaningful congressional oversight of federal agencies, under the theory that the departments and agencies of the federal government operate solely under the president's control. As I've shown at the beginning of this book, he has already used unpublicized "signing statements" to inform agency heads that they did not need to comply with reporting requirements mandated by Congress when it authorized federal activities or provided funds for management of the agencies and their programs.)

One could see the performance of the Bush administration as sufficient evidence of the dangers inherent in creating the kind of stronger executive office the president advocates, but there are other rejoinders to this claim that the nation requires a "super" presidency that would essentially eviscerate the constitutional assignment of legislative authority. The first is to consider whether in a time of substantially greater threat, during which there is a potential for unimaginable catastrophe in the event of miscalculation, the capacity for rapid-fire decision-making is the only, or even the most important, consideration, or whether the much higher stakes and much greater risk increase rather than reduce the need to act prudently as well as swiftly. What if prudence were to be sacrificed for the sake of expediency and the United States were one day to find itself engulfed in a war of possibly marginal value fought with insufficient advance preparation, inadequate supplies of troops and equipment, and no clear policy for extrication?

The second involves whether placing almost unchallenged domestic authority in the hands of a single individual substantially increases the need to ensure that only men or women of demonstrated decision-making and managerial competence be appointed or elected to positions of authority. What if a president were elected whose own limitations or skewed priorities caused him to appoint people of limited experience and questionable skill to high-level positions in which their subpar performances might result in serious mismanagement of disaster relief operations in the event of a hurricane, perhaps, or in managing the reconstruction of a war-ravaged nation?

In other words, a concentration of power in the presidency makes the election of a subpar president far more dangerous than election of a president limited in his or her ability to do harm. And such an expansion of authority would actually increase the likelihood of subpar performance by removing from the president the salutary effects of having to justify and defend his appointments and policies.

And yet, empowered by a stunningly acquiescent Congress and a conservative political movement that had abandoned its own principles in the pursuit of political power, President Bush, during the first six years of his presidency, pursued a vigorous expansion of presidential power unrivaled in American history. Taking the nation to war while keeping Congress largely in the dark, dictating the treatment of war captives (despite constitutional language clearly reserving that right to Congress), repeatedly signaling his intent to disregard legislation that he himself had signed into law, and deliberately disobeying other laws (for example, laws setting clear conditions before the government could eavesdrop on American citizens), the Bush administration has actively pursued the establishment of an American monarchy. In his poem "Ozymandias," Percy Shelley gives a portrait of an ancient autocrat who ruled imperiously ("with a sneer of cold command") and whose legacy was utter ruin, a lesson well worth remembering.

President Bush may have set new standards of disdain for competing authority, but the problem has not been one entirely new to his administration. The executive branch of government has been growing for years. When Franklin Roosevelt was president, he had a White House staff of 45. By the time Gerald Ford was president, the staff had grown to 533, and under President George H. W. Bush to 605. New Executive Branch departments and agencies have come into existence: the Central Intelligence Agency, the Equal Employment Opportunity Commission, the Office of Management and Budget, the Environmental Protection Agency, the Occupational Safety and Health Administration, the Defense Department, the Department of Energy, the Department of Education, the Department of Health and Human Services. Over the years, and particularly since 1945, Congress had consistently added to the responsibilities vested in the executive, from the transfer of the obligation to devise a comprehensive federal budget (an authority that was passed on to the president in 1921), to the concentration of economic expertise with the creation of an Executive Branch Council of Economic Advisors after World War II. John J. Pitney Jr., of Claremont College, recalled these expansions of presidential power in an article in the May 2000 issue of *Policy Review,* noting that the National Security Council, created by Congress in 1947, would consist "only of executive officials . . . reporting to the president." And, Pitney added, "Congress did not take the parallel step of reorganizing its relevant committees." From that point on, the national defense had become an area almost completely dominated by the White House, even though a good many defense-related issues are constitutionally assigned to Congress.

As the executive branch grew in power, assumed or assigned, the dangers that might flow from a presidency that felt unconstrained by the laws or the Constitution grew exponentially. In part this is because it is far easier for the press to focus attention on a single person—the president—than on 535 legislators. Most members of Congress, even the most powerful, remain virtually unknown outside their home states, whereas Americans are fed a steady diet of presidential pronouncements, making it far more risky for legislators to oppose presidential initiatives. As presidential scholar James MacGregor Burns wrote in his book *Leadership*, time has "transformed the role of the president into . . . the imperial and even the omnipotent presidency."

One need not look far to see the results of this presidential ability to reach into every part of the nation's life. Throughout the Bush presidency, Democratic members of Congress have repeatedly found themselves challenged in their home districts by constituents who had been subjected to a steady dose of White House claims that criticisms of the Iraq war were "unpatriotic" and damaging to American troops. Members of Congress who had questions about the war, or about other presidential actions, were often on the defensive until the tide turned and in 2006 the public reversed course, turned against the war, and turned Congress over to the very Democrats who had been buffeted for so long by gusts of presidential rhetoric.

In May 1974, E. Howard Hunt, who had recruited four of the five burglars who broke into the Watergate complex and created the scandal that brought down Richard Nixon's presidency, told *People* magazine that he "had always assumed, working for the CIA for so many years, that anything the White House wanted done was the law of the land." Thirty-three years later, almost to the date, *Washington Post* columnist David Ignatius described his conversations with "prominent GOP operatives . . . most of them high-level officials in the Reagan and Bush I and Bush II administrations." One, whom Ignatius described as "a prominent conservative," complained: "With this White House, there is loyalty not to an idea, but to a person."

There is an arrogance that settles into a White House—not a personal arrogance but a smugness born of the belief that no matter what the Constitution says, the executive is in charge, and everybody else's job is to fall in line. In both the Reagan and first Bush administrations, Republican members of Congress were often told bluntly by the president's enforcers that they were expected to toe the mark. Rich Bond, who later became chairman of the Republican National Committee, once threatened congressional Republicans that if they failed to follow White House marching orders, he would "cut them off at the knees." Bush's chief of staff, former New Hampshire Governor John Sununu, had a similar habit. Presidents are naturally inclined to take command. And yet the Constitution places power—real and considerable power—elsewhere. And it does so deliberately.

To a large extent, limiting the powers of the presidency relies on the president's own understanding of constitutional constraints. In our time, the presidency comes equipped with fleets of private aircraft and helicopters and squads of advance men and speechwriters, all dripping with ostentatious trappings of monarchy. It is perhaps understandable that modern presidents have sometimes come to think of themselves as elected royalty. But it is critical for us to remember that it's not so. There is a danger in a willingness to heave to whenever a president or a presidential underling breathes a desire.

How, then, to square the claim that the complexity of modern government and the threat posed by modern weaponry require a strong president with the dangers inherent in allowing the accumulation of unchecked authority in the hands of a single powerful leader? The answer may be found in the work of the late Richard Neustadt, a Harvard professor who specialized in studies of the presidency. Neustadt had worked in the White House during the Kennedy administration and was very much an advocate of strong presidents. But he defined presidential strength as an element of character: presidents gained their strength, he said, from the ability to win people over by the force of both their arguments and their personalities. It was reputation and prestige, not secrecy and placing oneself above the law, that gave presidents their power.

When Reagan and George H. W. Bush leaned on congressional Republicans to support positions they thought important but that ran counter to the positions the legislators, and perhaps their constituents, preferred, Reagan and Bush got the legislators' sympathy, but the constituents got their votes. Later, when Bill Clinton was president and his fellow Democrats held sizable margins in the House and Senate, he attempted, in his early years in office, to shape programs within the administration and count on members of his party to fall in line. But it was not to be that easy: Lee Hamilton, the Democrat from Indiana who was then chairman of the House Foreign Affairs Committee, told the *New York Times*, "I don't get elected because of what Bill Clinton thinks or what the House leadership thinks. The electorate makes up its own mind. That inevitably means that presidents have a lot less clout with Congress."

Presidents much prefer to gather analysts in the White House to develop policy and then send the presidential proposal to Capitol Hill to the roar of cannons and the thunder of drums. But government is not about analysis, it's about politics, and Congress, if it does its job, will play a significant role—if pushed, the dominant role—in setting the nation's course. A wise president will work within the system of separated powers, using his powers of persuasion, skill at negotiation, and an openness to compromise to influence public decisions. Theodore Roosevelt famously referred to the "bully pulpit" of the presidency; by virtue of the prominence of his office, a president, Roosevelt recognized, was in an especially good position to speak out on behalf of his policy preferences. "Bully," however, was a popular expression of Roosevelt's time meaning "splendid" or "superb"; it was not, as some more recent presidents have seemed to think, a platform from which to bully the people or their representatives.

Presidents and their underlings can bluster and threaten, but unless a member of Congress is unwilling to exercise the responsibilities of that office, presidential bluster won't amount to much. An old fable tells of a contest between the wind and the sun to see which could first force a man to shed his coat. The wind huffed and puffed and blew as hard as it could, and the man simply pulled his coat more tightly around him. The sun merely beamed warmth; off came the coat. But for some, huffing and puffing simply comes more naturally than warmth.

To be effective, presidents must be leaders, not self-proclaimed "deciders." And they must understand their own limitations, personally and constitutionally, and work to bring others on board. A president must work diligently to persuade. One may very well be a strong—that is, persuasive and effective—president without dismantling the walls separating the spheres of federal authority.

That is the answer to the dilemma. In the modern age, the United States needs a strong *president*, a man or woman with the ability to inspire and lead. What it does *not* need—indeed, what it should fear—is a strong *presidency*, an office invested with extra-constitutional powers that would transform the White House into a royal palace. Ironically, it is under a self-described conservative president, supported for most of his presidency by a conservative congressional majority, that this danger finally became very real.

In 1998, at the height of Clinton's legal battles in the Monica Lewinsky affair, I wrote in my weekly newspaper column, "Presidents are not above the law; the secret service is our police force, not his; while certain communications to the president regarding policy options may be protected from outside inquiry, the president's assistants are public, not personal, employees." I could not have foreseen that Clinton's successor would take an even more expansive view of the presidency and believe even more strongly that a president is above the law. "If the president orders it, it's legal," seems the Bush doctrine, as when he unilaterally declassified government documents (despite clear federal declassification procedures) during the prosecution of White House assistant I. Lewis "Scooter" Libby over his misleading of investigators who were looking into the "outing" of CIA operative Valerie Plame.

A president is, in the end, a public employee, holding a job others have held before him and that others will hold after he is gone. Legally, an elected public official—president, court clerk, member of Congress, or coroner—is the equivalent of a shoe salesman, burger flipper, track star, or homebuilder. So far as the right to justice is concerned, none of our fellow citizens, no matter the size of their salaries or the frequency with which they appear on television, is beyond the reach of the nation's laws.

During the Lewinsky affair, commentators protested that it would be somehow unseemly—an embarrassment to the United States—for the president to be hauled before a magistrate and forced to explain his conduct. One observer said that the president was the symbol of the United States and that the matter reflected on us all. But that was nonsense. The game of baseball is a symbol of the United States. So is the film industry. So are the Capitol dome, the Washington Monument, and the New York Stock Exchange. But not Bill Clinton and not George W. Bush.

In the movie *Amistad*, when Joseph Cinque, an African who has been kidnapped and sold into slavery, meets John Quincy Adams, a former president, he is told that Adams is a great American chief. Not so, replies Adams; he is a *former* chief. Once a chief, always a chief, says Cinque. Would that it were so, says Adams. Our chiefs—presidents, senators, representatives, governors, mayors—do their jobs and move back into the fold. They speak at conventions, teach classes, shill for commercial interests. In Washington, one can spot former government leaders walking down the streets, going in and out of local restaurants or movie theaters, standing in the checkout line at the grocery store. Residents of Boston are accustomed to seeing Michael Dukakis, a two-term governor of Massachusetts and the 1988 Democratic presidential candidate, riding the subways.

This is no small matter. It is, in fact, a restatement of the essential truth of America's commitment to limited government. The people will choose from among our number a few men and women to help manage the collective affairs of the nation. We will grant them a limited degree of authority, keep a close eye on them as they go about their—and our—business, and then send in somebody else to take their place. If we forget that no one is above the law, we will have lost rather than conserved the America that the founders created.

In the 1960s, comedian Pat Paulsen promoted his faux campaign for the presidency by saying on a popular evening television show, the *Smothers Brothers Comedy Hour,* "I don't want to be any more than I already am—a common, ordinary, simple savior of America's destiny." Paulsen, though, was joking. The founders feared nothing more than the accretion of power, which is why they so constrained government's freedom of action and gave the people's representatives the right to approve or disapprove of the chief executive's adventures.

In a *New York Times* editorial column in January 2007, Adam Cohen made the case for congressional action to impose restrictions on the White House. At the time, Bush was asserting ever more authority, most notably over the use of presidential signing statements and the treatment of captured enemy combatants, despite clear constitutional language placing that authority in the legislative branch. He had just told interviewers on CBS's *60 Minutes* that despite any action that Congress might take to limit his authority, "I've made my decision and I'm going forward with it." Cohen wrote, "The Founders, including James Madison, who is often called 'the father of the Constitution,' fully expected Congress to use these powers to rein in the commander in chief." He then quoted Madison, who summed up the founders' fears: "The constitution supposes, what the History of all Governments demonstrates, that the Executive is the branch of power most interested in war, and most prone to it. It has accordingly with studied care, vested the question of war in the Legislature."

Cohen cited a series of court decisions. In 1799, when President John Adams ordered U.S. ships to block sea traffic into and out of a French port, the Supreme Court ruled that it was unlawful, even during hostilities, for a president to take military action beyond what Congress had authorized. In 1952, the Supreme Court ruled that President Harry Truman could not seize the nation's steel mills, even during wartime, because Congress had ordered a different approach to settling steel mill strikes. During President Bush's own term, the Supreme Court declared the president could not establish military tribunals unless they followed congressional guidelines.

When President Bush declared that he was "going forward" with his Iraq plans no matter what Congress might do, he was not merely posturing or being "bold" or "decisive," as his supporters would have it. He was deliberately and consciously violating both the Constitution and a series of Supreme Court decisions reaffirming the right of the people themselves, through their representatives, to set limits on waging war. Even Kennedy and Lyndon Johnson, the two presidents most responsible for U.S. involvement in Vietnam, and both vehemently attacked by earlier conservatives, never came close to George Bush in defiance of Congress, the courts, and the Constitution.

It is frightening to contemplate—and more frightening to observe, as Americans have for nearly eight years—a White House in the hands of a man who so clearly does not understand, or so adamantly refuses to accept, constitutional limitations on presidential power. If one sees Congress as an interloper, a mere buttinsky-without-portfolio, as President Bush apparently does, it would be easy enough to justify the increasingly larger transgressions that undermine constitutional government.

On May 8, 2007, a group of Republican members of Congress met with President Bush to express their concerns about the management of the Iraq war and the concerns that the war—and Bush's low ratings—would prove damaging to the party. Afterward, several members of the delegation met with reporters outside the White House and discussed what they had told the president. One member of the group was Representative Ray LaHood, who had been in Congress since the day George W. Bush first became governor of Texas and who had been a representative in the Illinois legislature and chief of staff to Bob Michel, the Republican leader in the House of Representatives, when Bush's father was president. Another participant was Congressman Mark Kirk, also of Illinois, who was in his fourth term in the House. Kirk had flown missions in Iraq, Panama, Kosovo, and Bosnia; had been a naval intelligence officer; had worked at both the World Bank and the State Department; and had earned a master's degree from the London School of Economics and a law degree from Georgetown.

A May 11 headline in *The Hill*, a Capitol Hill newspaper, reported that Bush's staff members—staff members!—had attacked LaHood and Kirk for having the temerity to talk to the press. According to the report, a staff member named Dan Meyer, who was Bush's liaison to the House of Representatives, confronted LaHood and, with Karl Rove, a college dropout and the principal architect of a strategy that had Bush setting near-record low approval ratings, "rebuked" and "admonished" Kirk. Tony Snow, the president's press secretary, more forgiving of perceived misbehavior, remarked somewhat condescendingly that "when they get into a situation like that, they're excited about the prospect that they . . . have the opportunity to speak . . . with the president." The incident summed up in a nutshell the White House view of president as monarch.

In 1797, after serving for eight years as America's first president, the nation's first commander in chief, George Washington, having refused the title of "Your Majesty," walked away from his job and returned to his country home at Mount Vernon. In so doing, he established the most important precedent in all of American governance. Many Americans, influenced by sloppy teaching and lazy journalism, have come to think of a president as America's leader. But America has no national leader. In other countries a single person may be both head of state and head of government. The president of the United States is indisputably the head of state, the one American who merits a twenty-one-gun salute and the full honors accorded to the person who represents America on the world stage. But he is not the head of government; he is merely the head of one of three co-equal branches of government (and if one branch of government is, constitutionally, a little more equal than the others, it isn't his). That America's president is limited in his authority to act arbitrarily and is as subject to the laws as the rest of us is Washington's greatest legacy. It is that legacy we must conserve.

III

CONSERVATIVE VALUES

VALUE #1: FREEDOM

C ONSERVATIVES today would have us believe they are the voice of American values. In fact, they are not even the voice of conservative values.

At its core, conservatism embraces a philosophy of freedom. More libertarian than prescriptive, it is inherently protective of individual rights and resistant to concentrated power, wherever it might be found. There have always been conservatives who see themselves first and foremost as defenders of a particular set of social traditions—as a kind of morality police—and conservatives who see themselves as political operatives for the corporate boardroom, sometimes failing to draw the distinction between entrepreneurship and competitive free enterprise on the one hand, and protected market share on the other. In many respects, those kinds of conservatives are indistinguishable from liberals: they believe in using the power of the state to protect or advance favored interests.

I have defined "conservatism"—American conservatism specifically—as a political philosophy that traces its roots to John Locke's recognition of the inherent dignity of the individual (citizen, not subject). From that source flow freedom of conscience (and religious practice), freedom of speech, freedom of assembly, and so forth—the building blocks of American democracy. Most modern conservatives pay considerable lip service to this philosophy but undermine it by the policies they advocate.

Consider their many attempts to amend the Constitution, to turn it into little more than a set of local ordinances applied to the nation as a whole. Rather than allowing individual communities (the proper repositories of "community standards") to determine acceptable, or protected, behavior, or whether to permit activities that, whether laudatory or repugnant, have no adverse effects on non-participants, many of today's conservatives (like the political correctness police of the Left) would dictate to citizens and communities alike what kinds of behavior should be allowed. In his 2007 memoir, *The Age of Turbulence*, Alan Greenspan quoted Ronald Reagan: "Government exists to protect us from each other. Where government has gone beyond its limits is in deciding to protect us from ourselves." It is a distinction that has apparently been lost.

Churches may properly proscribe certain practices and declare them beyond the scope of their religious doctrines, but America is not a church. Any political movement that holds itself up as a champion of liberty betrays its own principles when it dictates the terms of *political* acceptability. *I Love You, You're Perfect, Now Change*, the title of a Broadway show, is an apt description of the attitude many of today's conservatives have toward the Constitution. They honor—even revere—it for its groundbreaking commitment to the protection of individual rights, yet many are eager to rewrite it with language designed to turn the Constitution on its head, increasing the government's power, limiting liberties, and imposing their own beliefs.

Proposed constitutional amendments centered on the homo-sexual/heterosexual divide have attracted much attention in recent years. So has the ongoing public debate about abortion. Because both are such "hot-button" issues, it may be helpful to consider instead a proposed amendment that is, at the moment, less radioactive: a constitutional prohibition against burning the American flag.

I confess to a particularly strong attachment to the flag. As a child, I devoured books about the American Revolution and placed pictures of Nathan Hale, Patrick Henry, Ethan Allen, Francis Marion, and other Revolutionary War heroes on my bedroom wall. As an editorial-page columnist for the *Chicago Tribune*, I was thrilled to see the statue of Nathan Hale outside the *Tribune*'s Michigan Avenue offices. Like many Americans, I was disturbed by television broadcasts showing students setting the American flag on fire.

But there is a profound difference between being bothered by the behavior of another and legally prohibiting it. What separates the United States from so many other countries is the right of its citizens to criticize their government, even when they do so in offensive ways. Harvard Square is not Tiananmen Square. In America, protest is permitted (and, if Thomas Jefferson's words can be believed, encouraged). Burning the American flag may be offensive, but it is not an insult to those who died defending what it stands for, which includes the right to say what one wishes about the government.

Some conservatives would protect the flag by requiring that citizens show reverence for it, thereby, while professing their love for freedom, imitating those totalitarian regimes in which if you insult the leader, tear down the flag, or raise your voice in protest, the government will swoop down with swift and sure punishment. There are many ways to protest government policies, and burning the flag that is the nation's symbol may be particularly offensive, yet in the end it is just that, a symbol. The freedom to protest, on the other hand, is not symbolic; it is the essence of a free society.

Conservatives today sometimes seem to be deliberately attempting to undermine and discredit conservatism and its constitutional values. Many are not content merely to advocate the behaviors they favor and criticize lifestyles they oppose—actions well within the framework of America's protected liberties. Rather, they are increasingly willing to enforce their preferences by proscribing lifestyles that diverge from their own. A system of government that was designed to protect the rights of the minority is now seen as a weapon to force minorities to conform to the views of the majority. This is not American conservatism, no matter what label the cultural homogenizers may choose to put on it.

Another example of the willingness to employ the power of the state against the individual involves attempts to root out the remnants of the once-pervasive drug culture. It is a goal with which I sympathize. During my years in Congress I, too, was concerned about the exposure of children to addictive drugs, and I supported stiff punishments for drug dealers who pushed their products into the public schools. But the concern should be for the victims and the punishment for the criminals. In the mid-1990s, the Supreme Court authorized the government to conduct random drug testing of student athletes, even when there was no reason to suspect drug use. Many conservatives were delighted even though the power of the state had been turned not against the criminal but against the potential victim. The Constitution is not vague on this subject: it protects our freedoms by refusing the government the right to conduct unreasonable searches. We are presumed innocent; we do not surrender the protections of the Constitution when we decide to play football. If the government can now subject American citizens to police searches without cause in the name of the public concern of the moment, then it is we, not the drug dealers, who will have lost the war. Yet such an expansion of state power was cheered most loudly by many who would pretend to claim the inheritance of a movement founded on a belief in maximizing freedom.

There are other examples. Conservatives have long believed in free enterprise, an entrepreneurial, competition-based activity, the economic equivalent of political liberty. Today, many have become champions of gigantic corporations that attempt to limit competition and that take their primary goals to be not the improvement of product and service but the maximization of profit and salary. They have worked to protect corporations from lawsuits and to oppose a patient's rights in dealing with medical practitioners. These conservatives have become almost knee-jerk defenders of the big against the small, the merchant against the purchaser, the corporation against the citizen.

But nowhere was the abandonment of conservative values more clear than in the erosion of the separation of powers. A *New York Times* article in September 2006, headlined "Shifting Power to a President," described legislation that set standards for the treatment of detainees in the attempt to block terrorist attacks on the United States and to pry information from prisoners captured in Iraq or Afghanistan.

Here the issue was not one of congressional somnolence; Congress eventually acted, albeit at the president's request, and gave him what he had asked for. Nor was it a matter of presidential overreaching. Though President Bush had fiercely resisted attempts to limit his unilateral policymaking, an adverse Supreme Court ruling (in *Hamdan v. Rumsfeld*) made clear the need for prior congressional authorization, and so he asked for, and received, legislative permission to do what he had been doing in the first place. Plus a few additional powers: the conservative-dominated Congress granted him the authority to determine the meaning and application of the Geneva Convention standards for the treatment of war prisoners and, slapping the Supreme Court for its effrontery in insisting that the president remain faithful to the Constitution, stripped the federal courts of their jurisdiction to hear challenges to his decisions.

The result was to turn the system on its head. As the *Times* described the resulting legislation, "In effect, it allows the president to identify enemies, imprison them indefinitely and interrogate them . . . beyond the reach of the full court reviews traditionally afforded criminal defendants and ordinary prisoners. Taken as a whole, the law will give the president more power over terrorism suspects than he had before (the *Hamdan* decision)."

There is no question that the terrorist threat is real and that the United States must act sensibly to protect itself. The issue is how to balance security and liberty, how to construct a national defense that retains the essence of what makes America free and unique. The legislation sought by a conservative president and granted by a conservative Congress put all its emphasis on security and none on the preservation of liberty. The president was granted the authority to determine who shall be considered an "enemy" and what behaviors will lead to that designation; the legislation authorized keeping in prison indefinitely persons who had neither been convicted of, nor even charged with, a crime—precisely the kind of arbitrary "star chamber" powers that were so repellent to the founders, who insisted that the right of habeas corpus (which would prevent such indefinite imprisonment) not be abridged.

One might well argue that the extraordinary circumstances of the time—stateless and hidden terrorists determined to kill as many Americans as possible—justify unusual counter-methods. Our enemies are actively seeking to repeat the horrors of September 2001. Clearly, we must be equally aggressive in countering the threat. But not with the creation of a de facto defense dictatorship. Belief in the rule of law is the very essence, the sine qua non, of a free society. In 2006, however, conservatives in Congress and in the White House turned their backs on the constitutional separation of powers and the rule of law, adopting as their new approach to governance the granting of arbitrary authority.

For more than a dozen years, people who call themselves conservatives have claimed to be the champions of a "values-based" politics. What has changed fundamentally is what those "values" are. They have not merely evolved since the days of Barry Goldwater; they have been reversed. If conservatives oppose individual choice, favor limitations on speech, and persistently side with the wealthy and against the maintenance of a fair playing field for economic competition, then what values are they championing? Certainly not conservative values.

VALUE #2: PEACE

The Constitution was written by individuals intimately familiar with the propensity of European monarchs to send their subjects off to die on foreign battlefields. If the "walls" built into it have any overriding objective, it is to prevent the same thing from happening here. The United States might indeed choose to go to war, but that decision would be made not by a single political leader but by representatives of the people themselves. In a document that far exceeded the practices of most other contemporary societies in limiting central authority, there was no more striking departure from the norms of the day than deliberately withholding from the chief executive the power to declare war. No American could be sent off to fight, and possibly to die, unless the people themselves determined that the cause was one that was worth the cost.

Reluctance to go to war is also a central tenet of American conservatism. The Left demonized conservatives as advocates of an aggressive militarism, but they missed the point, just as today's conservatives have missed the point. When scholars like Russell Kirk and Clinton Rossiter attempted to reduce the fundamental tenets of American conservatism to a few basic principles, one of the first was "prudence," an innate caution; conservatives were obsessed with looking both ways before crossing any policy street. Their operating premise was, "If something can go wrong, it probably will." (Kirk listed prudence as "chief among virtues," and Rossiter listed stability, continuity, and peace as the marks of a good society.)

Conservatives are not, and never were, America's sunny optimists, certain that if one acted boldly enough, things would turn out well in the end. During the Democratic Party's stranglehold on Congress from the mid-1950s to the mid-1990s, Republicans almost reflexively responded to every proposal for a new federal activity by advocating "pilot projects," testing ideas carefully at state or local levels before accepting changes that would affect the entire country. Conservatives were the nation's worriers. They did not share the belief that the Soviets could be reasoned with: they feared the shoe-pounding dictators in Moscow and fretted about the emergence of potential Kremlin allies. And they worried that if the United States were perceived as militarily weak (as had been the case before both World War I and World War II, when the nation had allowed its defenses to shrivel), that perception might well invite an overconfident Soviet Union to launch an attack on western Europe and initiate World War III.

Support for a military buildup was designed not to advance the cause of war but to deter it. The conservative mantra then was "peace through strength." And although nonconservatives countered that a military buildup would in itself be sufficiently provocative to cause a war rather than deter it, conservatives supported a powerful military force because they *believed* it was the best way to preserve peace.

That is precisely the point that today's conservatives seem not to have grasped. Although the isolationist wing of conservatism (fearful of entanglements that could lead to war) has mostly disappeared, the conservative abhorrence of war, and the high value placed on prudence, should have put conservatives in the forefront of those attempting to slow down the rush to war in Iraq. They should have been the president's most aggressive skeptics, demanding information about plans for reconstruction and an eventual withdrawal from the country, challenging estimates of the numbers of troops required and the resources they would need. And, above all, they should have been persistent in insisting on incontrovertible proof of the dangers that Iraq posed before agreeing to send young American men and women to battle; it was, after all, precisely to protect against such military adventurism that the Constitution's authors had taken the power of war away from the chief executive and put it in the hands of the people.

Instead, congressional conservatives were reluctant to challenge presidential demands. Since the beginning of the war in Iraq, President Bush and members of his administration have periodically attempted to challenge the patriotism of those who demanded answers. But it is conservatives who have failed to live up to their own principles: prudence may indeed sometimes dictate taking military action, but only after much more serious consideration than today's conservatives are willing to invest. Conservatives never constituted a war party; rather, they were determined to keep the United States strong enough to ensure that its citizens would not have to face death on distant battlefields. Conservatives now have a much harder time claiming to be a "peace" party; they have shown a singular unwillingness to embrace the fundamental prudence that would make such a claim credible.

Ironically, before the confluence of a Republican presidency and Republican control of Congress, conservatives were far more willing to follow their traditional emphasis on prudence. Though they wanted to keep the United States militarily strong, they recognized a difference between strength and profligate spending. In the 1990s, the Air Force made a commitment to the deployment of the F-22 radar-evading fighter, and Congress earmarked nearly $2 billion to build the first six planes. But the Pentagon was not satisfied; it wanted lots of other things as well, including other fighters, more helicopters, and more ships. And Congress—the Republican, conservative Congress—decided it was time to draw the line. By an overwhelming vote, the House canceled funding for the plane's production—this after the previous, Democrat-controlled Congress, had killed only one warplane in the production stage in nearly half a century.

And that was the second congressional slap at the Pentagon in a matter of a few days. When the annual Defense Appropriation Bill reached the House floor, it was accompanied by a report issued by the conservative majority denouncing the Pentagon for financing programs not approved by Congress. The report accused the military of both illegal and unconstitutional acts, one of which was the Pentagon's penchant for "re-programming"—switching funds from a program for which money had been approved to another—without first seeking approval or even notifying Congress of the switch.

This is the understanding that has disappeared from the conservative ranks in Congress. Conservative belief in peace through strength was of a piece with the conservative propensity for prudence and fiscal responsibility. Wars were to be avoided if at all possible, entered into only after all the arguments in its favor had been rigorously examined and forcefully challenged. The United States would enhance the prospects for peace by maintaining a military capability that was second to none, but that did not mean blindly pouring money into an insatiable military-industrial complex.

In May 2007, senior editor Howard Fineman commented in *Newsweek* magazine about the attempts by presidential candidates in both parties to settle on an approach for dealing with the war in Iraq and the challenge posed by the reality of (in Rudy Giuliani's words) "the fact that there are really dangerous people who want to come here and kill us." Republicans, Fineman said, "are choosing to focus on fear." And Democratic candidates, in his view, were still floundering, trying to simultaneously satisfy antiwar activists and reassure the broader public of their ability to protect the nation. Fineman wrote that if the candidates in either party were searching for a role model, they needed to look no further than the setting for an upcoming GOP debate: the Ronald Reagan Library. For all his rhetoric, Fineman wrote, Reagan was cautious about the use of military force. In 1982, after sending Marines on what proved to be a deadly mission to Lebanon, Reagan had taken a closer look at the situation in the Middle East and called the troops home.

Ronald Reagan was serious about national security. He wanted to build space-based weapons that could intercept Soviet missiles before they reached the United States. He was forceful in his challenges ("Mr. Gorbachev, tear down this wall"). He moved the United States from the long-standing "containment" policy formulated by George Kennan to a new "rollback" approach, putting the Soviet Union on the defensive whenever he could. He encouraged indigenous attempts to overthrow Soviet-friendly regimes. Reagan was certainly not passive, and he was not hesitant to do what he thought necessary to keep America safe. But he pushed aggressively in support of his dream of a nuclear-free world, enlisting the Soviet Union in a commitment to draw down the two nations' stockpiles of nuclear weapons. And he was, as Fineman points out, "cautious about military force," willing to use it when he thought it necessary but not eager, not bellicose, not ready to charge off to war.

For a while, conservatives remembered that. And then George W. Bush became president, and the challenges, the examinations, and the insistence on peace and prudence were suddenly discarded as casualties of Congress's inexplicable abandonment of its constitutional responsibilities.

VALUE #3: FAITH IN THE COMMUNITY AND THE INDIVIDUAL

Alexis de Tocqueville noted the very high degree of religious belief among this new nation's citizens. Whether in the founding of the new universities (Harvard, essentially a divinity school, was first), or denouncing witchcraft or banding together to build silos and steeples side by side, this was a land of believers. And the country remains a nation in which churchgoing and religious faith are strong components. Yet America has always kept religion at arm's length from public decision making. It is common for men and women elected to the nation's highest offices to profess strong faith— "Thank you, and may God bless America" has become the semi-official last line of political speeches—but generally sectarianism remained outside the building when policymakers sat down to set priorities or establish community budgets. The wall between church and state remained standing.

Reacting to the tendency of some secularists—abetted, at times, by the courts—to marginalize religious expression, some have pointed out, accurately, that the Constitution contains no specific language mandating the separation of church and state. Rather the opposite, they argue: the "establishment clause" of the Constitution is designed not to be dismissive of religion but to protect it: "The Congress shall make no law respecting an establishment of religion." In other words, when it comes to religion, Congress has no authority and should butt out. It is the government that should keep its distance from religion, not the other way around.

But walls have two sides. The establishment clause keeps religion on one side of the wall and government on the other. In a nation of more than three hundred million people, there are a great many faiths (almost all of them professing to be the repository of ultimate truth) and a great many people who subscribe to none of them. For adherents to a particular set of religious beliefs to translate those beliefs into policy, and those policies into laws that all must obey, would be as much a betrayal of the Constitution as would Congress mandating that a particular sect be given state-supported preferences.

This wall, too, is being undermined. Attempts to prohibit abortion are generally based on religious belief; those who advocate legislation that would overturn state election results and prevent doctors from helping terminally ill patients end their suffering base their policies on scriptural interpretations; attacks on the use of human stem cells for research are often based on religious beliefs. It is one thing, of course, for policymakers to arrive at these positions on other grounds—competing priorities, cost-benefit analyses, even communitarian concepts of mutual support—but something entirely different when religious belief guides decision making on public questions. Walls are two-sided, and swords are double-edged. To use religious conviction to make policy decisions is to run the risk that far different religious convictions will someday shape the laws. Once the idea of sectarian lawmaking is acceptable, there is no going back.

The wall between religion and statecraft serves an additional purpose. The enemy of civility (a necessary ingredient in the governance of a diverse society) is certitude. And nothing breeds certitude more than religious belief. Religion is often a positive force in the lives of individuals, but when the true believer feels compelled to impose upon the whole of the society the truths that have enriched his or her life, the threads that bind us as a nation begin to fray. The congressional battle over whether to intervene to prevent the removal of life support from the comatose Terri Schiavo (which I'll discuss in detail later) was fueled in part by religious belief. The extraordinary lengths to which congressional and administration Republicans went in trying to overturn an Oregon state law that permitted physicians to assist the terminally ill in ending their suffering was based on similar arguments.

There has been much debate in recent years over the proper role for religion in the "public square"—that is, in the arena in which laws are written and policies established. Many proponents of religion-based governance argue that in the past half-century there has been an undermining of American culture and tradition; they point to the removal of the Ten Commandments and Christmas displays from public sites and a ban on prayer in classrooms and even at high school sports events. As time passes, and policymakers and judges pass from the scene, some of the contested decisions may be revisited. But these are legal matters to be fought within the confines of the Constitution and subsequent statutes, not on the grounds of a policymaker's religious beliefs.

Conservatism's central philosophy has long been based on the regard for the individual rather than the collective. Yet today many are willing to support the imposition of the personal beliefs of some, be they a majority or a minority, on others who do not subscribe to those beliefs. The title of Sinclair Lewis's novel about a politician who rose to power on a wave of religious fervor was ironic: *It Can't Happen Here*. Its message was: yes, it can.

VALUE #4: THE RULE OF LAW

For decades, as political and social activists sought to use the courts to help them achieve victories they were unable to win in the legislative arena, American conservatives articulated a clear and consistent principle: the federal courts, they said, were not meant to be a part of the *political* system. Even though Supreme Court Justices and lower-court federal judges attained their positions as a result of having been selected and approved by elected public officials, they were to be guided not by their own philosophies and political preferences but by the law.

To distinguish between proper judicial behavior and judicial usurpation of the legislative role was critical. "Activist judges," conservatives said, attempted to impose their own (predominantly liberal) social visions by engaging in tortuous distortions of clear constitutional language. Conservatives demanded the appointment of "strict constructionists": judges who would adhere to the actual wording of the Constitution without creative interpretations of what the founders "really meant" or what they would have meant had they been able to foresee life in the modern age.

Though this was a narrow interpretation of the judicial function, it was nonetheless a position based on sound legal principle. The

Constitution provides a mechanism for establishing public law (there are roles for both Congress and the president), two separate procedures for revising the original language, and a way to replace lawmakers (elections every twenty-four months). Thus, conservatives could argue, judicial activism was not only outside the scope of the judiciary's constitutional mandate, it was also unnecessary. Admittedly, these procedures to bring about change might be slow, but, conservatives would say, a prudent society should proceed deliberately when bringing about fundamental restructuring either politically or socially. Judicial constraint might have serious social consequences (certainly a system of racially segregated schools should not have been allowed to continue until the public was ready to endorse a change) but at least conservatives could argue that their concern was not over outcome but process. The courts simply did not have the authority to act as super-legislatures, no matter how desirable the result. (And in the case of the segregated schools, no judicial overreaching was required; such separation of citizens into racial categories was a clear constitutional violation.)

Today, many conservatives have either lost sight of what "strict construction" actually means or have themselves become ardent proponents of judicial activism. The most famous example of this transformation is Robert Bork, whom Reagan nominated to the Supreme Court in 1987. Bork became a conservative hero when his confirmation was denied after a campaign led by Senator Edward Kennedy and a broad coalition of liberal activist organizations. Bork described himself—and was described by others—as an "originalist," somebody who believed the judiciary was bound to decide constitutional questions according to the intent of the founders.

To that extent, Bork did indeed represent conservative thought. "Strict construction" and "originalism" seek to interpret the Constitution by its own clear language, with any ambiguities to be resolved by reference to the founders' intentions. Bork was outraged by the Supreme Court's ruling in *Roe v. Wade*, which upheld the right to abortion ("a woman's right to choose") based on an implied right to privacy. "We are increasingly governed," he said, "not by law or elected representatives but by an unelected, unrepresentative, unaccountable committee of lawyers applying no will but their own." Many conservatives, most of whom were likewise opposed to abortion, saw Bork's criticism of the decision as both principled and courageous.

It was also a model of confused reasoning—and certainly not, in any sense, "conservative." Consider his complaint that the Court's decisions were made by "unelected" and "unrepresentative" lawyers. In fact, the conservative position had long been that the Constitution was a document designed to limit the ability of both rulers and majorities to impinge on the rights of individuals. To suggest that judicial rulings should conform to the majority will (through "elected" and "representative" implementers of that will) was to deny the very essence of conservative thought. Were judges elected, and representative of the views of the majority, then popular sentiment, not the Constitution—and not the law—would guide them. American constitutional government would have been strangled by those who most loudly proclaimed their love for it.

Bork's views were most pronounced in his statements outlining the reasons for his opposition to *Roe v. Wade*. In commenting on the Court's earlier decision in *Griswold v. Connecticut*, which formed the basis for the *Roe* decision, Bork wrote: "[Justice] Douglas did not explain how it was that the Framers created five or six specific rights that could, with considerable stretching, be called 'privacy,' and, though the Framers chose not to create more, the Court could nevertheless invent a general right of privacy that the Framers had, inexplicably, left out." According to Bork, the framers of the Constitution had spelled out within that document the rights retained by American citizens, and that any rights that the founders had not spelled out simply did not exist. But this formulation ignores the Ninth and Tenth Amendments, which make clear that any rights not specifically delegated to the federal government remain with the states and the people. Moreover, it is a complete repudiation of the conservative principle that it is government powers, not citizen rights, that should be limited. Judge Bork misunderstood the single most important—and most conservative—provision in the U.S. Constitution: unless we have specifically delegated them to the government, our rights remain ours.

Although the Bork nomination would be considered only by members of the Senate, and the opinion of a member of the House of Representatives was thus of little importance, I took the opportunity at a breakfast meeting in the Capitol to ask Bork whether he had been misquoted. No, he replied. Those were indeed his views; the American people, he believed, had only those rights assigned to them under the Constitution. It was a view in extreme opposition to long-established principles of the American conservative movement.

From then on, it became common for conservatives to call for the impeachment of judges with whose rulings they disagreed. Even though the Constitution envisions impeachment only in rare instances of misbehavior or crime—a limitation designed to protect the judiciary's independence—House Majority Leader Tom De-Lay, Senator Rick Santorum (then the chairman of the Senate Republican Conference), Phyllis Schlafly, and the editorial writers of the *Washington Times* all joined in the campaign to remove judges for failure to rule in accordance with what they perceived as public opinion (so much for "strict construction"). Ironically, some of the rulings these conservatives found so troubling *did* reflect majority opinion. Conservatives had twisted themselves into such a tangle that they were now simultaneously attacking judges for *not* following public opinion and seeking to remove them because they *were* following public opinion. All sense of restraint had disappeared.

Today conservatives seem to have lost interest in preserving the walls that maintained the separation of powers. The Republican-controlled Senate confirmed the appointment of both John Roberts and Samuel Alito to seats on the Supreme Court even though both appear to hold an expansionist view of presidential power. As expected, Senate Democrats and liberal advocacy groups waged aggressive challenges to both nominations. But conservatives should have confronted the nominees with hard questions of their own, given writings in which both Roberts and Alito argued for concentrating more power in the White House. If conservatives truly believed in preventing the accumulation of power—the bedrock principle of both the Constitution and American conservatism—Roberts and Alito should have been pressed as to whether they agreed with the president's use of signing statements to assert a right to disregard the law, or his claimed authority to disobey laws already on the books (such as the requirement for court-issued warrants before citizens could be subjected to electronic surveillance), or his belief in a "unitary executive" authority that limited congressional oversight and would bar Congress from setting qualification standards for the heads of federal departments and agencies. But the challenge from conservatives never materialized.

Conservatives will no doubt continue to insist *publicly* on a judiciary that sticks strictly to the limits of the Constitution. But strict adherence to an agenda, not strict construction of the Constitution, has become the rallying cry. Late in 1996, long after his nomination battle, Judge Bork resurfaced with a book in which he called for censorship to curb speech that offended him, and he endorsed allowing a simple majority vote of Congress to overrule the Supreme Court. Bork now seems to favor a dictatorship of the masses, precisely the kind of democracy that both Plato and Madison most feared: public opinion would trump constitutional constraint, and liberty would be at the discretion of the popular vote.

Because the Constitution's central premise is liberty—it is a document designed for a free people—it was created to prevent *both* the concentration of power in a few hands (thus the limits on the executive) and the ability of the majority to impose its will on the minority (thus limits on what government may do, even with the support of the majority of citizens). The rule of law, not the rule of masses or rulers, defines American constitutional government. But that is a lesson conservatives have forgotten.

VALUE #5: JUSTICE

There is another important wall in the constitutional framework, that between politics and justice.

In 1982, Jerry Miller was charged with rape. He was tried and convicted, and he was sentenced to prison. A quarter of a century passed while Miller, who was not yet 25 when he went behind bars, lost his youth and spent his days living with the dangers and the indignities of prison life. Few conservatives, myself included, shed tears over the fate of those sentenced to live behind bars. Prisons aren't country clubs, and if the victims of a crime—if they survive— must forever live with the memory of what was done to them, why should we worry whether a criminal has access to salad bars and television sets? But as it turns out, Jerry Miller was a victim, too. In April 2007, twenty-five years after he was arrested, Miller's conviction was overturned when DNA evidence proved he was an innocent man.

Since 1989, according to the New York–based Innocence Project, Jerry Miller was the two hundredth person who was found to have been wrongly convicted of a crime. Lawyers at the Innocence Project did a little math and determined that the two hundred people who had been convicted of a crime they didn't commit collectively spent 2,475 years in prison. According to a press release issued by the Innocence Project when Miller was released, "Nobody knows how many innocent people are in prison. Only a small fraction of cases involve evidence that could be tested for DNA and even among those cases, evidence is often lost or destroyed before it can be tested."

Conservatives are famous for being "tough on crime." A compassionate society will think first and foremost of those who have been crime's victims. To favor strict penalties is not only a defensible proposition, but, if there is indeed a deterrence effect, reducing the likelihood of future crime, it is the only reasonable response.

But if the *wrong* person is convicted, the wrong done to the victim is not avenged, the wrongfully convicted is unjustly deprived of life or liberty, and the true criminal remains free to commit crimes against more victims. Nonetheless, conservatives, who are often the most skeptical of government competence, almost routinely side with law enforcers (local police, FBI agents, prosecuting attorneys). This tendency to defer to government officials in this area while being wary of them in others has a further irony. Conservatives tend to believe in the free market in part because they believe in the efficacy of a reward system. But that should lead conservatives to be more cautious about too quickly accepting the pronouncements of the police (whose reward system is too often based on numbers of arrests) and prosecutors (whose reelection or reappointment is often based on securing convictions). For conservatives, protecting individuals against false arrest and false imprisonment should be a prime concern.

Columnist George Will has persistently pointed out the dangers of the current "law and order" system of pursuing justice. As he wrote in a *Washington Post* column about the death penalty, "Capital punishment, like the rest of the criminal justice system, is a government program, so skepticism is in order."

"In the 24 years since the resumption of executions under Supreme Court guidelines," Will wrote, "about 620 have occurred, but 87 condemned persons—one for every seven executed—had their convictions vacated by exonerating evidence. . . . One inescapable inference from these numbers is that some of the 620 persons executed were innocent."

Indeed, much has been reported about failures of the American justice system, including numerous cases of persons convicted as a result of mistaken eyewitness identification or of grossly incompetent representation by poorly qualified defense attorneys.

None of this constitutes an argument against capital punishment as a legitimate legal and social response to particularly heinous crimes. Might not justice be best served by ensuring that a killer cannot kill again? Might not society, by forfeiting a killer's life, reaffirm the value of the life the killer took? But conservatives need to remember that it is not conviction but *justice*—the fair, impartial, and proper conviction and sentencing of the actual perpetrator of a crime—that benefits society. Conservatives should be the leading proponents of any legislation designed to ensure that the accused receive adequate representation, that systems are established to make a greater number of arrests and convictions less of an incentive for police and prosecutors, and to provide DNA testing whenever it might help determine guilt or innocence in any capital punishment case. Indeed, in October 2007 the *New York Times* reported that "all but eight states now give inmates varying degrees of access to DNA evidence that might not have been available at the time of their convictions." In addition, the article said that many states have begun to reform crime lab procedures, the ways in which witnesses are used to identify suspects, and the use of police informants. Obviously, the evidence indicates that a great gap sometimes exists between conviction and justice.

The pursuit of justice may carry significant emotional baggage. This is where a commitment to justice and individual rights puts conservatives to the test. Can one stand for principle even when doing so strains one's most basic instincts? Five examples come to mind, two from the distant past, one from the more recent past, and one very much with us today.

(1) In November 1734, a New York publisher named John Peter Zenger was arrested and charged with seditious libel. Zenger was, in fact, guilty. His newspaper, the *New York Weekly Journal*, had persistently attacked the royal governor of the time, William Cosby. The law at that time (forty-two years before the colonies declared

their independence from Great Britain) was clear: truth was no defense against a charge of libel. It was sufficient for prosecution that Zenger had "inflamed" the public's mind "against His Majesty's government," which Zenger had clearly done. Alexander Hamilton defended Zenger, but Governor Cosby, who was bringing the suit against Zenger, exercised his right to appoint the judges. A traditionalist European conservative would have certainly condemned Zenger for his disruption of the public order and his calumny against an official of the royal government. But choosing between following the law and doing what was "just," the jury of colonial citizens declared that despite the law and the prohibition against attacking government officials, the fact that Zenger's claims were true was a defense against the government's prosecution. Thus was born the freedom of the press and the right of citizens to criticize, forcefully, their government.

Many of today's law-and-order conservatives would side against rabble-rousers such as Zenger, but his acquittal represents a crucial moment in American history. It was very much a result that a pro-liberty conservative would have applauded.

(2) Thirty-six years after Zenger's acquittal, another trial tested the colonial sense of justice. On March 5, 1770, eight British soldiers, part of a force occupying Boston, fired into a group of local citizens, killing five. This came to be known as "The Boston Massacre." The soldiers were arrested and brought to trial. Their defense was not one likely to elicit much sympathy from colonists who were already irate over the presence of British troops and the heavy-handed rule of a distant government. Charged with murder and tried in a city clamoring for the death penalty, the soldiers were defended by one of the most famous American colonists of all, John Adams, later to be the new nation's second president. Witnesses testified that the mob of Bostonians had surrounded the soldiers, shouting, "Kill them, kill them." Ultimately, the men were convicted of manslaughter rather than murder, and they were freed. Again, it was not vengeance that prevailed; it was justice.

(3) A few years later, when Adams was president, the issue involved was not civil or criminal action but legislation. In 1798, fearful of a war with France, Congress passed and Adams signed four bills that came to be known collectively as the Alien and Sedition Acts. The most controversial were the acts that gave the president the authority to deport—in peacetime—any noncitizens considered "dangerous to the peace and safety" of the nation; the one that allowed the government to arrest, imprison, and deport anybody who was a citizen of a foreign power with which the United States was at war (still the law today); and, finally, the one that called for the imprisonment, on grounds of treason, of any person convicted of "false, scandalous, and malicious writing" about the government (twenty-five men, most of them editors of newspapers supporting Adams's rival, Thomas Jefferson, were arrested and thrown into prison).

The Alien and Sedition Acts represent a dark moment in American history, when innocence or guilt was collectively assessed and when any criticism of the government constituted a sufficient basis for arrest and imprisonment. The idea of "liberty," proclaimed so ardently in the Declaration of Independence and formalized in the Constitution, was set aside at the first whiff of danger. It was not the last time Americans would overreact to threat by deciding constitutional "niceties" were inconvenient. Today, as we weigh how best to respond to the threat of stateless terrorism, the temptation to put the Constitution aside is constant; what our enemies cannot do to us, we may do to ourselves.

(4) This example, though some seventy years old, still burns white-hot in the minds of many Americans. Norman Yoshio Mineta, a congressman and later a cabinet secretary under both President Bill Clinton and President George W. Bush, had something more than party affiliation (Democrat) or legislative service in common with his fellow congressman Robert Takeo Matsui. Both had been placed in internment camps as children during World War II, victims of a fear that Japanese Americans would engage in espionage

and sabotage against the United States. In fact, more than 120,000 persons of Japanese ancestry, more than two-thirds of them U.S. citizens, were rounded up and placed in camps. The camps were established under Executive Order 9066, issued by President Franklin Roosevelt on February 19, 1942, less than three months after the Japanese attack on Pearl Harbor. According to a later report by the War Relocation Authority, the internees were housed in "tarpaper-covered barracks . . . without plumbing or cooking facilities of any kind." In 1988, forty-three years after the end of World War II, Congress established a fund to pay the victims who still survived $20,000 each as minimal compensation for the property they had lost.

Like the Alien and Sedition Acts, Executive Order 9066 was not a rogue act. Both were passed by Congress, signed by the president, and upheld by the Supreme Court. In both instances, the denial of liberty, the overreaching of government, and the setting aside of constitutional protections were carried out according to the book. And were thoroughly unjust.

Which brings us to the most recent example—one clouded by fear and driven by a legitimate instinct for self-preservation.

(5) During the wars in Iraq and Afghanistan, the United States military took a number of prisoners and placed them in various detention camps, most notably at Guantanamo and Abu Ghraib. Military interrogators sometimes used force or threat in questioning prisoners. In every case, the military refused to allow the prisoners basic due process rights, including the right to be formally charged, to be told of the charges against them, and to have the right to challenge those accusations. At first, the lack of due process was simply mandated by the White House. When the detainees filed habeas corpus petitions (asserting the right to challenge their detention in a legal proceeding), the Supreme Court ruled first that they had a right to a hearing and later that the military commissions under which the president wanted them tried were a violation of both international law and the United States' own Uniform Code of

Military Justice. At which point the president got a conservative-dominated Congress to pass legislation authorizing the military commissions and stripping the detainees of their habeas corpus rights.

Legally, the issues involved are far from clear-cut. The Fourteenth Amendment to the Constitution declares that the privileges and immunities of American "citizens" may not be abridged, but it goes on to say that no "person" may be deprived of life, liberty, or property without due process of law. Nor may "any person" within the relevant jurisdiction be denied "the equal protection of the laws." Legal scholars are of very different minds as to whether the distinction between "citizens" and "persons" is significant. The issue is whether the framers meant only "citizens" in both cases or whether they wanted to make clear that a just legal system will ensure that nobody is denied due process and equal protection.

The issue is further complicated by a simple, rational, consideration. The United States is at war with an enemy dedicated to its destruction. The military and the White House argue that giving enemy prisoners an opportunity to hear the evidence against them and to challenge it may reveal too much information about how we know what we know; in a war such as this, they argue, compromising intelligence-gathering procedures is a risky business.

The dilemma for conservatives, however, is that liberty and justice are intimately linked. They are both rights to which any individual is entitled. One has a right not to be deprived of life or liberty without the ability to challenge the power of the state. This is the basis on which Alexander Hamilton defended John Peter Zenger when he was accused of libeling the king's appointed governor of New York; it is the basis upon which John Adams defended eight British soldiers after the Boston Massacre; it is the basis upon which Thomas Jefferson declared that the Alien and Sedition Acts were unconstitutional and issued pardons for everybody convicted under them; and it is the basis upon which the American Congress formally apologized to Japanese Americans for their treatment during World War II.

No right is more central to liberty than that of habeas corpus. As I've pointed out, the founders were familiar with a Europe in which kings and tyrants could simply arrest enemies, rivals, and critics and throw them into prison without charges or trial. Article 1, Section 9, of the Constitution states that "the privilege of the Writ of Habeas Corpus shall not be suspended, unless when in cases of Rebellion or Invasion the public Safety may require it"—the basis on which Lincoln suspended it during the Civil War.

Justice is not an easy concept to grasp: it involves fairness and, sometimes, compassion, but in many cases it may also carry a steel rod; "to do justice" and "to love mercy" may not be the same. Nonetheless, the search for justice and the commitment to justice are essential components of the American experiment. The Constitution is more than a grab-bag of separate elements, and what holds it together are the first eighteen words of the Constitution: "We the People of the United States, in Order to form a more perfect Union, establish Justice . . ." Justice is at the very top of the list and in the same paragraph that declares the nation's commitment to "secure the Blessings of Liberty."

Testifying before the U.S. Senate in January 2007, former attorney general Alberto Gonzales, in one of the more jaw-dropping statements ever issued by a senior public official, said, "There is no expressed grant of habeas in the Constitution; there's a prohibition against taking it away."

"Wait a minute," protested Arlen Specter, chairman of the Senate Judiciary Committee. "The Constitution says you can't take it away except in case of rebellion or invasion. Doesn't that mean you have the right of habeas corpus unless there's a rebellion or invasion?"

"The Constitution doesn't say every individual in the United States or citizen is hereby granted or assured the right of habeas corpus," Gonzales replied. "It doesn't say that. It simply says the right shall not be suspended except in cases of rebellion or invasion."

Specter was apoplectic. "You may be treading on your inter-diction of violating common sense," he told Gonzales.

Merely violating "common sense" is far too generous an inter-pretation. Gonzales, who has been portrayed as hopelessly beyond his depth, was, in fact, neither stupid nor naïve, but he was dan-gerous. His assertion—a denial of the Constitution's clearly ex-pressed prohibition against the government holding people in prison indefinitely, without charges or the right to argue for their release—is of a piece with a disturbing tendency among some conservatives to deny the very existence of even the most funda-mental constitutional guarantees. It is eerily similar to what Robert Bork argued during his confirmation hearings: unless the Con-stitution clearly and explicitly assigns a "right" to the people, that right does not exist, and therefore there is nothing to prevent the government from doing whatever it pleases. Like Bork's, Gonzales's twisted formulation—a ban on suspension of the writ of habeas corpus does not mean that there is a right to habeas corpus—is in clear contravention of the Ninth and Tenth Amendments.

Like all Americans, conservatives must make a choice: whether or not to set aside constitutional protections in the face of threats to the country's security. But without individual rights, there is no United States, and without justice, there is no liberty. Sometimes, it takes courage to stand for the principles that form the basis of the liberty that conservatives have long held as America's most precious promise.

VALUE #6: RESTRAINT

America's relations with the rest of the world have never been simple. George Washington famously warned of the dangers of "entangling alliances" with the competing powers of eighteenth-century Europe. But John Adams, Washington's vice president and successor, and Thomas Jefferson, Washington's secretary of state and Adams's successor, didn't heed Washington's warnings. Neither hesitated in choosing sides in the endless and often bloody European rivalries; Jefferson was resolutely pro-France, whereas Adams's sympathies were with the British. The Alien and Sedition Acts that Adams signed were aimed primarily at Jefferson's pro-France allies.

By the time the United States had inaugurated its fifth president, James Monroe, the nation was less shy about playing on the world stage. Having twice defeated Great Britain in wars and having seen both Spain and France retreat from North America, the United States was now ready to start asserting itself internationally. Monroe warned the Europeans that this country would not stand idly by if they attempted to expand their presence anywhere in the Western Hemisphere. The Monroe Doctrine pledged "neutrality," but only if the Europeans kept their distance.

In the space of a single century after Monroe's 1823 declaration, the United States had waged war against both Spain and Mexico and had become a part of the alliance that defeated Germany in World War I. Woodrow Wilson had persuaded Congress to enter the European war not because America itself was in danger of attack but so the world would "be made safe for democracy." Alliance followed alliance. Over the next fifty years, the United States entered NATO and now-defunct, NATO-like military alliances, such as the Southeast Asia Treaty Organization (SEATO) and the Middle Eastern–based Central Treaty Organization (CENTO). It pledged to defend the Republic of China, established on the tiny island of Formosa after its leaders had been driven from the Chinese mainland. It established military outposts, just as Rome had done, throughout the world. Americans fought in Korea and Vietnam. All of these "entangling alliances" were part of an expansive foreign policy that was designed, as president George W. Bush later described it, to enable the United States to take on its enemies "over there" before we had to fight them "over here."

Maintaining neutrality has been impossible. For one thing, there really is evil in the world, more than purely the result of competing interests and misunderstandings. There are and have been leaders willing to subdue other nations and massacre millions of innocents to achieve their purposes. Forswearing the use of military force is not an option for any people who wish to remain safe or free.

Given the many options for engaging a world filled with potential enemies, what policies should conservatives determine appropriate? Devising effective foreign policy strategies and building the necessary alliances that will stand the test of time should be the goal rather than merely dealing with the exigencies of the moment and engaging in a never-ending series of expedient but ultimately short-sighted stopgap policies.

The answer lies in a rejection of the foreign policy approaches that have dominated conservative thinking for the past several decades. One, the interventionist policy so ardently pursued by neoconservatives, is based on an obsession with the virtues of democracy and a commitment to democratizing the world one way or another. Both Plato and Hegel may have been wrong in the depth of their disdain for democracy (Plato considered it the worst possible form of government other than tyranny), but as Fareed Zakaria has observed, America's concern should be for the spread of *liberal* democracies, with their embrace of not only free elections, but free choice, a free press, independent courts, and a respect for individual rights. Democracy by itself, merely the ability of a majority to choose its leadership, may actually produce governments at odds with concepts of liberty and justice. The United States is itself not a pure democracy, but a mediated, constrained democracy in which the powers of elected leaders and the people are carefully circumscribed.

Once one embraces Zakaria's view, as all conservatives should— after all, our political philosophy holds "liberty" as its ultimate aim—the nostrums of the neoconservatives seem hopelessly simplistic and even dangerous. In the days leading up to the U.S.

invasion of Iraq, the Bush administration argued that war was necessary not because Saddam Hussein's Baathist tyranny was an affront to human values, but because Saddam's arsenal of unconventional weapons posed a distinct threat to American security. Only later, when it was revealed that there were no weapons of mass destruction hidden in Iraq, and that Saddam's regime had not been on the verge of producing such weapons, did the president fall back on the argument that building a democracy in the Middle East was in and of itself sufficient justification for the war.

Like the old American Communists, who switched positions whenever new directives came out of the Kremlin, the neoconservatives moved from supporting the war as a preemptive move (that is, hit the enemy before he hits you) to defending it as a preventive move (hit the enemy just to make sure he can't later hit you), to praising it as a means of reshaping the entire Middle East by showing Iraq's neighbors how governing should be done. It was a hopelessly naïve policy for a number of reasons.

First, though most conservatives—like most Americans—would likely support a policy of *preemption* (if America's enemies are on the verge of launching a deadly strike against the United States), *preventive* strikes stand on far shakier ground. There is a possibility that North Korea will send agents to New York to blow up hotels or office buildings. Perhaps Iran will do so. There is no indication, however, that such an attack is either likely to happen or imminent. Prevention is not preemption; it's about eradicating any potential future harm. With such a policy, the United States might find itself in one conflict after another for decades to come.

Second, anybody who believes that installing an elected government in Baghdad or Kabul will cause Saudi kings to abdicate, Jordanian kings to declare an end to Hashemite rule, or Egyptian strongmen to invite dissent is dreaming. Although I find it hard to understand why anybody would want to live without free choice and protected rights, there are many societies in which tradition and belief trump individual rights. In *Escape from Freedom*, Erich Fromm observes that there are circumstances in which the responsibilities of free choice may prove to be an "unbearable burden." In such cases, he writes, people are often driven to surrender their freedoms in exchange for a system that promises more security and less uncertainty. To assume that merely showing the flag of American-style democracy and individualism will cause millions of Muslims to abandon their theocratic impulses is naïve; to send Americans off to war, and death, in such a belief is madness.

American conservatism rests on a tripartite foundation: a belief in liberty, ensured by constraints on government; belief in the value of prudence in both action and decision; and a commitment to peace, including the willingness to spend large sums of money to create a military sufficient to deter potential enemies. The neoconservative approach to foreign policy eschews prudence, is impatient with constraint, and is all too willing to engage in war. Their viewpoint, both shortsighted and naïve, is wrongly ascribed to the conservative movement which it has infiltrated but not absorbed. Unfortunately, President Bush and others in Congress have been all too willing to accept the neoconservative approach as a way of dealing with threat.

Aristotle defined virtue as the avoidance of extremes. In foreign policy, however, it has been the embrace of extremes that has predominated, with the United States lurching back and forth between naïve idealism (the neoconservative approach) and Realpolitik pragmatism. If neoconservatives are driven by theoretical objectives, and by a moral or ethical compass that fails to take into account the complexities of world politics, adherents to a Realpolitik foreign policy often seem to have no moral compass at all, single-mindedly pursuing their ideas about the American national interest with no concern for the nature of those governments or national leaders with whom the country might ally itself. Thus it was that in seeking ways to solidify the West's defense against Soviet expansionism, the country that Ronald Reagan often described as a "shining city on the hill," a beacon of freedom, found itself supporting brutal dictatorships in Iran, Nicaragua, and Cuba. It stood with oligarchs in Panama, El Salvador, and Guatemala. It resisted the imposition of economic sanctions against the apartheid regime in South Africa. It stood firmly behind Chiang Kai-shek's ruling Kuomintang Party on Taiwan, whose leaders believed they could hold government offices in perpetuity or until voters on the now-Communist mainland were somehow given the opportunity to reelect or replace them.

In a single-minded pursuit of short-term interests, we repeatedly looked away as freedoms were denied and people were persecuted. In *Demien*, Hermann Hesse wrote that Europe had conquered the world only to lose its soul. The point is a good one: nations, like people, can lose their souls. What makes America unique is not the mere fact of its existence but that it exists as a nation committed to the principles of freedom. To acquiesce in the denial of liberty is a crime against everything that Americans—and conservatives—most fervently believe in. In addition, American support for foreign dictatorships will almost inevitably result in turning the people of those countries against the United States, seeing this country as complicit in their oppression. America has both practical and moral reasons to desire the spread of freedom and the protection of human rights.

How, then, to shape a foreign policy that truly complies with conservative ideals? One that is neither thoughtlessly adventurous nor blind to American values? Here are some starting points squarely within the ambit of the conservative political perspective:

First, recognize limits: forswear the temptation to become the world's Chief Buttinsky. Unless a government poses a serious threat to American security or American interests, the form of government within that nation's borders is none of our business. In concert with other nations, the United States sometimes feel compelled for humanitarian reasons to intervene in another nation's internal affairs, but a government's ideology should not matter. Whether a people choose a socialist government or one more in line with Western free-market capitalism is their concern, not ours.

How far the United States has drifted from awareness of its own limitations was made clear in November 2006 when Daniel Ortega was elected president of Nicaragua. Ortega and the United States have a bit of a history. In 1979, in the midst of the Cold War, Ortega deposed Nicaragua's dictator, Anastasio Somoza, one of those oligarchs the United States had supported. A self-described Marxist revolutionary, Ortega allied his new Sandinista government with the Soviet Union, and the United States, first under Ronald Reagan and then under George H. W. Bush, launched an effort to topple him by providing support for a guerrilla opposition movement. The U.S. involvement centered on fears that the Sandinistas would undermine neighboring Central American governments and provide a base of operations for the Soviets.

That was then. Eventually international pressure forced the Sandinistas to submit to an election, monitored by outside observers. In 1990, Violetta Chamorro, a Managua newspaper publisher whose husband had been murdered by the Somoza regime, defeated Ortega and ended the country's decade-long leftist experiment. For the conservatives who had supported the Contra effort, it was a great victory. I had spent many hours with Chamorro in her offices at *La Prensa*, the family-owned newspaper in Managua, and was part of the U.S. delegation to her inauguration as Nicaragua's president. It was an intensely satisfying moment.

Sixteen years later, after four unsuccessful attempts to regain the presidency, Ortega ran yet again. The United States attempted to influence the election outcome by warning voters that if Ortega won, it might cut off all aid to Nicaragua, one of the region's most impoverished countries. Ortega did win, handily, over the Bush administration's preferred candidate, Eduardo Montealegre, at which point the administration warned Ortega that it would keep a close eye on him to ensure that he maintained a suitably democratic government.

When the United States faced the risk of war, perhaps even a planet-destroying war, against the Soviet Union, it mattered greatly to American security interests whether its adversary had an ally in the region. But the Soviet Union is gone. Though the United States has the right to provide assistance only to governments that it approves of, whether Nicaraguans or the citizens of any other country choose to live under market capitalism or socialism is none of our business And whether a country chooses to live under a system of constrained and divided powers, as the U.S. system was meant to be, or one in which power is more centralized (the British parliamentary system, for example), or one in which authority is tightly controlled is, again, that country's business, not ours.

The Ortega story demonstrates that we have allowed the virus of intrusiveness to infect our foreign policy almost to the extent of becoming a part of our national DNA. But active interference in the domestic affairs of other nations is thoroughly inconsistent with the most fundamental of conservative principles: prudence. Ours is a philosophy of limits. We may choose which nations to support with aid and which to forge trade agreements with, but attempting to pick another nation's leaders is a clear mark of an imperialist mentality and is a policy that no conservative should support.

Second, with the overriding objective being peace—something for which previous generations of conservatives were willing to make great sacrifice—conservatives should insist that the use of military force be America's last option, not its first. We are fortunate; the United States is a wealthy country and the combined resources produced by American ingenuity and diligence have provided its leaders with a vast array of tools when it comes to our national security. Joseph Nye, the former dean of Harvard's Kennedy School of Government, has written of America's arsenal of "soft power," including a multibillion-dollar foreign aid program, a huge reservoir of technical know-how to help other nations battle poverty and disease, and a massive diplomatic corps.

Conservatives have always been aggressive about protecting American interests. A conservative's natural sense of caution leads him to be alert to potential threats, but there are many nonmilitary options available to America's leaders. Military force may counter threats, but it is a threat in and of itself; its use weakens the country both militarily and economically, and the cost in American lives is high. It would be foolhardy to write off war as an option, but it is equally foolhardy to engage in war before other means have been exhausted.

American conservatism resides on the twin pillars of a belief in liberty and constraints on centralized power. Nothing should be more offensive to the determination to keep government in its place than the specter of the government sending thousands of young men and women off to foreign battlefields. The true conservative will insist on a process whereby war will be waged only with the *properly informed* consent of the people.

When President Bush's father launched the first Gulf War against Saddam Hussein's Iraqi army in 1991, the evidence justifying war was far more persuasive than when his son decided on his war against Saddam. Operation Desert Storm was a direct response to the Iraqi invasion of Kuwait, a provocation so egregious that thirty nations joined the U.S.-led military coalition. Yet even under those circumstances, with most of the democratic world agreeing on the war's necessity, Congress performed its constitutional responsibilities carefully and deliberately.

As a senior member of the House Republican leadership and chairman of the party's Policy Committee, I inherited the task of helping Congressman William Broomfield, the ranking Republican member of the Committee on Foreign Affairs, in managing the floor debate in support of the resolution authorizing the war. During my sixteen years in Congress, I was never prouder of the entire national legislature, House and Senate, Democrat and Republican, than during that debate. Approval of military action would have been the first such congressional authorization for the use of force since the passage of the Vietnam-era Gulf of Tonkin resolution nearly thirty years earlier. We all felt the weight of the decision. Young Americans, perhaps a great many of them, would die.

The debate raged for three days but was marked by a loftier and more sober demeanor than is common in most legislative combat. In the end, the Senate approved going to war by a narrow margin of 52–47; the House voted to authorize military action, 250–183, only after adding a condition that required the administration to exhaust all diplomatic options before sending troops into battle. Congress had ensured that the decision would rest, ultimately, where the Constitution placed it: in the hands of the people. Both the House and Senate were controlled by Democrats and liberals in 1991, but the course they followed was a classically conservative course: liberty demands a tight rein on the ability of any "national leader" to plunge a nation into war. President Bush received the war authorization he had requested (though, it should be noted, after first attempting to argue that he did not need Congress's approval to send the nation to war).

Although the immediacy of the need was less apparent, the vote to enter the second Gulf War was comparatively cursory. With Republicans now controlling both the House and Senate, and a Republican in the White House, there was far less scrutiny of the arguments advanced for a military strike. Later, Democratic Congressman John Spratt—a member of the House Armed Services Committee who had voted in favor of the first Gulf War, supported the Patriot Act, supported Reagan's space-based defense system, and even supported a resolution declaring the Iraq war to be a part of the greater worldwide "war on terror"—complained that although there had been extended hearings before the 1991 vote, there had been nothing similar prior to the overwhelming vote eleven years later to give the president authority to launch the current war.

It bears repeating: conservatives are, at base, constitutionalists and believers in the separation of powers. All this is fundamental to how they engage the world. America's relationship with the rest of the world is based more on commercial exchange and the shaping of terms for trade than on military conflict. In Article 1, Section 8, the United States Constitution assigns to Congress the authority and responsibility "to regulate commerce with foreign nations." Yet nowhere has the abdication of congressional power been more egregious than in international trade agreements. Presidents retain authority over the negotiation stage of international treaties, but under the Constitution nothing then can occur—no agreement negotiated by the administration can take effect—unless the people, through their representatives, concur. In the case of treaties, the Senate must give its approval. In the case of other compacts, such as the North American Free Trade Agreement, which created considerable political controversy during both the first Bush and Clinton administrations, both the Senate and the House of Representatives must agree to the terms. NAFTA was controversial for good reason: trade agreements may seriously affect the viability of a wide range of American enterprises, from cattle ranchers and wheat farmers to auto manufacturers and steel mills, and they may directly influence jobs, job protection, and employment benefits. American social and labor policies implemented by Congress over decades may be summarily reversed by the terms of international trade agreements.

Given the serious potential consequences of such international arrangements, and the desire to protect American sovereignty, a conservative would naturally insist on subjecting proposed agreements to the scrutiny and deliberation of the entire legislative process—from public hearings in both houses to thorough debate first at the committee level and then before the entire membership of the House and Senate, and then to full consideration of proposed changes. And yet in recent years, conservatives, including those most protective of American sovereignty (denouncing, for example, the prospect of American soldiers serving under NATO commanders from other countries), have been too willing to shirk constitutional responsibility and leave such decisions to the president and his inner circle.

This abdication—in the form of "fast track" proposals that would require Congress to accept presidentially negotiated trade agreements in their entirety, without change, or reject them altogether—undercuts one of the fundamental protections of liberty, the people's control over their own government. To remove Congress's ability to pass judgment on and amend the law is to undercut much of the power and purpose of the legislature as a separate and equal part of the national government. It is a surrender of constitutional authority that should be deeply disturbing to conservatives.

This is a global age, bringing enormous opportunities and significant challenges. The concept of the nation-state and the scope and limits of national sovereignty are undergoing dramatic re-evaluation. But the United States was founded on a set of certain fundamental assumptions that inspired generations of men and women to emigrate to its shores. Here was a land in which individual progress was predicated upon merit and commitment, not inheritance. Here was no king, no all-powerful circle of nobles, no ecclesiastical dictatorship. In short, the United States was a part of the circle of nations, but it was also something different. American "exceptionalism" was no myth; it had meaning.

There will be those who object to the claim of American "exceptionalism" because they believe it to reflect an arrogant assumption that Americans are superior to people who live in other parts of the world. But that's not what it means: the American idea is a different idea, and fundamental to it is a commitment to liberty. Liberty is dependent on—indeed, predicated upon—citizens' maintaining control of their own destinies, including deciding when to go to war and what their relation with the rest of the world should be.

In recent years, many conservatives have forsaken fundamental principles and increasingly accepted "might makes right" as an operating principle—endorsing American intrusion in the affairs of other nations and attempts to shape the world to their liking. Instead of being reluctant warriors, they have taken the nation to war after only the most cursory attempt at considering alternatives. They have abandoned prudence, constraint, and a sense of limits. They have surrendered their constitutional obligation to keep decisions about war and trade in the hands of the people.

VALUE #7: LIMITS

George Orwell may have coined the term "Big Brother" but he didn't invent the concept. By the time he wrote *1984*, four years after the end of World War II, totalitarianism was well advanced. But it was always somewhere else, somewhere different and distant. Franklin Roosevelt's opponents may have seen the aggressive expansion of the federal government during the 1930s as something equally sinister, but an all-seeing and all-controlling state was as alien to America, then as before, as were monarchy and hereditary aristocracy. America was about freedom, and that meant primarily freedom from the heavy hand of government.

Neither Orwell nor his contemporary Ayn Rand, author of *Atlas Shrugged* and *The Fountainhead*, was a native American (though the Russian-born Rand did become a U.S. citizen soon after coming to America). Neither Orwell (a British teacher and shopkeeper) nor Rand had been raised in a society shaped by a James Madison or a Thomas Jefferson. Orwell was, in fact, a fervent British leftist; Rand had spent her early years, into her twenties, living in Russia under both the czar and Stalin. Yet in the 1950s, with the Soviet Union posing a real threat to American survival and the United States government extending its reach into the affairs of its citizens, the Orwell-Rand warnings about the dangers of an omnipotent state struck a deep chord. Millions of Americans bought their books.

American conservatives, just coming of age politically in this environment, made containment of government their primary cause. Though few were as fiercely individualistic as Rand, they agreed with Goldwater that the central question to ask of each new government proposal was "Does it maximize freedom?" As a corollary to that proposition, they insisted on a firm division between the rights and powers delegated to the federal government and those retained by the states and local communities. In a sense, they were the descendants of the Revolutionary-era anti-Federalists, who feared that by singling out for special emphasis just a few of the rights that were beyond the purview of government, the Bill of Rights would leave the false impression that every right not named would be presumed to fall within the realm of federal authority. This fear of centralized government was the unifying theme of the emerging conservative movement: governments were a necessary evil, required both because it was sometimes necessary to protect the most vulnerable citizens from their stronger neighbors (men were not angels, Madison said; if they were, governments would not be needed) and because only a sufficiently strong central authority could provide a viable defense against foreign threat. But governments were to be the servants, not the masters, of the people. The people would have to be vigilant; government would have to be watched carefully.

With the heirs of this conservative tradition having now had the opportunity to shape public policy, one wonders what "vigilance" means. And whether today's conservatives recognize any limits at all on the legitimate reach of government. Increasingly, the federal government has extended its authority in ways that would have appalled earlier conservatives, ranging from attempts to require state and local law enforcement officials to act as de facto agents of the federal government (so much for the wall between federal and local authority), to efforts to overturn the effects of a public referendum approved twice by Oregon voters (in essence, insisting that terminally ill patients be required to go slowly and painfully to their deaths), to attempts to interfere with a medical decision approved by a patient's husband and doctors, to the creation of federal "watch lists," to electronic eavesdropping on citizens' telephone calls, and to the subversion of due process.

Ironically, even when the current administration has attempted to do the right thing, it has retained a belief in its ability to simply issue commands. When, in February 2005, the president "ordered" Texas courts to conduct new hearings for fifty-one prisoners on death row (all were Mexican-born and had argued that they were denied access to Mexican consular officials before being sentenced), the Texas Court of Criminal Appeals issued a stinging rebuke. The president, it said, had "exceeded his constitutional authority by intruding into the independent powers of the judiciary." As reported in the *Philadelphia Inquirer*, the court said that neither the Constitution nor any act of Congress had empowered the president to issue such an order. It may have been a moot point, however, since this president and the conservatives in Congress who support him seem disinclined to accept any presumption that presidents need constitutional or congressional authority.

Expanding the reach of the federal government into areas that have traditionally been left to the states has become all too common in modern "conservative" circles. In August 2006, members of the National Governors Association protested a move by the Republican-dominated House of Representatives to extend the president's authority to take over the National Guard in the event of a security threat or a natural disaster. The association's chairman, Arkansas's Republican governor Mike Huckabee, warned that the legislation would end the historic link between states and their National Guard units. The *Washington Post* quoted Huckabee as saying that the attempt to shift control of the National Guard to the president not only violated two hundred years of American history but was symptomatic of a larger federal effort to make states no more than "satellites of the national government."

Nothing better illustrates this new conservative belief in an unlimited central government than two cases that captured widespread public attention and turned the soul of American conservatism inside out.

The better-known case involved a young Florida woman named Terri Schiavo, who collapsed in her St. Petersburg home early in 1990 and was subsequently institutionalized. Doctors said she had fallen into a persistent vegetative state with no hope for recovery. In 1998, her husband, Michael Schiavo, attempted to have physicians remove the feeding tubes that had kept his wife alive for nearly a decade. To this point, the Schiavo case was simply another local tragedy. Ms. Schiavo's parents objected to the removal of life support and turned to antiabortion activist Randall Terry for help. In short order, the case was transformed into a political cause. Conservative members of the Florida legislature authorized Governor Jeb Bush to intervene; he did, ordering state officials to ensure that the patient's feeding tube remain in place. Conservative members of Congress did their part, too, going so far as to subpoena Ms. Schiavo, who could not talk or communicate in any other way, to testify before a congressional committee so that she could be taken into the federal witness protection program.

The American people were appalled by this blatant attempt to inject personal or religious ideology into what was a private medical decision. In an ABC News poll on March 20, 2005, fully 70 percent of respondents, including a majority who identified themselves as "conservative" or "evangelical," found government intervention into the Schiavo case "inappropriate." A CBS News poll the next day found that 82 percent of those polled, including 76 percent of self-identified conservatives, believed Congress should stay out of the issue altogether. A *USA Today*/CNN/Gallup poll at the beginning of April found that 76 percent disapproved of Congress's involvement. Perhaps the most telling rebuke to the White House and elected conservatives was the finding in the CBS poll that three out of every four persons polled believed that governments should "stay entirely out of end-of-life matters." It was the people, not the conservatives they had elected, who were embracing traditional conservative values.

The disturbing implications of the Schiavo case were nothing compared to the less visible but more far-reaching attempts to interfere with a state law in Oregon that permitted dying patients to receive medications that could help them end their terminal agonies. In this one case, those who posed as conservatives managed to turn their backs on three cardinal conservative principles: state preeminence in matters not constitutionally delegated to the federal government, respect for individual choice, and limits to government power.

In 1994, Oregon voters approved a statewide initiative authorizing what came to be known as a "death with dignity" law. It was a carefully drawn law that would allow patients to gain access to lethal drugs only under certain conditions. The patient must be certified to be terminally ill, with no more than six months to live. That prognosis would have to be confirmed by a second physician. The patient must be an adult and certified as mentally competent to make the decision to seek life-ending drugs. The patient must request the lethal medication verbally on two separate occasions at least fifteen days apart. The patient must also request the medication in writing, with the request witnessed by two other people who are neither health care providers nor related to the patient. And with all that, the patient retained the right to rescind the request at any time. Finally, no physician would be permitted to administer the lethal dose; doctors could only prescribe the medicines and deliver them to the patients, who would accept full responsibility for their use. Not only did Oregon voters approve the law once, but they also approved it a second time, overwhelmingly, three years later.

The reason for the law is simple: many terminally ill patients face deaths that are drawn out and extremely painful. Many lose the ability to control their most basic physical functions. Sometimes they choke to death. Agony, day after day, week after week, often marks the end of life. In these circumstances, some adults, knowing death is imminent, prefer to exit quietly and painlessly.

Many may disagree with the proposition that, even in such circumstances, ending one's own life is an acceptable option. There is, in fact, nothing in conservative political theory to dictate a proper answer to such a question. What there is, however, is the belief that, whatever choice one might make, it is not the role of the federal government to interfere. Having taxed and regulated and otherwise constrained citizens throughout their lives, it should not also mandate that they must die an agonizing death.

And yet that is precisely the position that was taken by both the Bush administration, purporting to represent conservative values, and the conservatives in Congress. Overriding the repeated decision of Oregon voters (in a matter clearly within the purview of the state, not the federal government), ignoring the most fundamental decisions of those citizens most directly affected, and stretching the boundaries of government far beyond anything the founders could have envisioned, today's "conservatives" tried with both legislation and bureaucratic directive to invalidate the death with dignity law.

The most blatant—and the most devious—attempts were undertaken by President Bush's attorney general, John Ashcroft. As a U.S. senator from Missouri, Ashcroft urged president Clinton's attorney general, Janet Reno, to block the Oregon law. She refused. So when Ashcroft was named to that position, he undertook that mission himself. Congress had enacted a federal statute called the Controlled Substances Act, which permitted the federal government to regulate the manufacture, importation, possession, and distribution of certain drugs. Even though the act was passed to assist in fighting the illegal drug trade, not to regulate medical practice, Ashcroft issued a directive declaring that Oregon doctors would face prosecution under the law if they provided the lethal medicines that patients asked for and that Oregon law permitted.

A federal court promptly blocked Ashcroft's ploy, declaring that his directive was unlawful, that it violated the clear language of the law he sought to use, that it "contravened Congress's express legislative intent," and that it overstepped "the bounds of the Attorney

General's statutory authority." It was precisely the kind of complaint that conservatives had once leveled against the Left. And the court was blunt in assessing the effect of what Ashcroft was trying to do: "Doctors will be afraid to write prescriptions sufficient to painlessly hasten death. Pharmacists will fear filling their prescriptions. Patients will be consigned to continued suffering and . . . may die slow and agonizing deaths." On January 18, 2006, with the new attorney general, Alberto Gonzales, representing the administration's position, the Supreme Court sided with the lower court, 6–3, finding the Bush/Ashcroft/Gonzales position unlawful.

This was not merely some rogue operation by an attorney general attempting to impose his own theological beliefs on a sovereign state. Ashcroft was not alone. In the House, Henry Hyde, chairman of the House Judiciary Committee, introduced a bill to block the Oregon law; it had 165 cosponsors, mostly Republican. A companion bill was introduced in the Senate. So long as the Oregon law remains on the books (more than two hundred dying Oregonians have taken advantage of the law to end their suffering), it is almost certain that Republican members of Congress will continue to seek ways to end the practice. And they will undoubtedly claim to be conservatives as they do so.

What a confusion this all makes. This is a nation in which politicians are trying to reshape the health care system, even at great cost, to ensure that no citizen suffers needlessly; how can such a nation also condemn many of its citizens to a slow, painful, anguished death? Authority is critical to maintaining an ordered society, but so, too, is it important that the exercise of authority be questioned and, when necessary, defied. The founding fathers designed a Constitution to keep the government out of those areas in which it does not belong. Commitment to those limits was, for many years, what defined American conservatives. One wonders whether today's conservatives believe in any limits at all.

A little more than ten years ago, when I was teaching a Harvard course on American conservatism, I was invited to serve as co-chairman of a seminar on conservative political movements in Western industrialized nations, a gathering of fifty scholars from thirty countries held in Salzburg, Austria. It was supposed to be a study of the principles we conservatives held in common. But in fact we had very little in common. The Salzburg Seminars are widely respected as conveners of scholarly discussions about a wide range of topics, but in this instance the assumptions were seriously flawed. As I've pointed out, American "conservatism" is essentially European "liberalism," emphasizing the individual rather than the state. In much of the world, "conservatives" are those who too often offer the clenched fist and shrill voice of ethnic nationalism or religious fundamentalism. What worried me somewhat then, and worries me far more today, is that American conservatism has itself begun to edge toward the European model of ethnic identity and prescribed values.

IV

STEPS TOWARD
RECLAIMING
CONSERVATISM

WHY DOES IT MATTER?

Aꜰᴛᴇʀ leaving Congress, I taught at Harvard for eleven years and have now taught at Princeton for four. I enjoy teaching, but in some ways, and most notably in the questions I ask, I'm a fish out of water. As somebody whose preparation for teaching was experiential rather than through a study of academic literature, I have a decidedly nonprofessorial concern for relevance. As a result of a speech I had given at a political science convention in Providence, I was invited by the American Political Science Association to contribute an article to its new journal, *Perspectives on Politics*, that illustrated the great gap between political science and politics itself. After presentations by visiting scholars or during faculty "work-in-progress" presentations, I would ask the ultimate nonacademic question: "So what? Even if what you say is true," I would ask, "what is its significance? Why does it matter?"

The same question is relevant here. Though it might provide a sense of satisfaction to outline the "truths" that once guided the conservative movement and to document the ways in which a new mix of philosophies—brashly interventionist, corporate, monarchical, theologically oriented—has displaced true American conservatism on the political stage, what of it? If this strange and disturbing hybrid that passes for conservatism today continues to be the conservatism of the future, what, really, will we have lost? After all, the world we live in is not the world of forty years ago.

This is why it matters: I believe we must either recapture the soul of American conservatism or we will ultimately destroy the country that the founders created, that the Constitution guaranteed, and that the rights of a free people demand. America will be "exceptional" no longer. Whether we were wrong to go to war in Iraq or have merely handled the enterprise in a criminally inept way, or both, that decision is now behind us. And if Congress failed to perform its constitutional obligations and neglected its oversight responsibilities, the people guilty of that dereliction of duty have been removed from power. The question now is, What will happen next time?

Preserving the peace has been a conservative goal. Modern American presidents from Kennedy to Reagan have been forthright in warning potential adversaries that we would "pay any price"—combat included—to preserve our national liberties, and conservatives fully embrace that obligation. But they embrace it reluctantly. As Russell Kirk noted, to conservatives, "prudence" is a virtue. Rushing to war without exploring every possible alternative is neither prudent nor virtuous. Conservative idealism does not exist in a vacuum, of course. It recognizes the reality of prospective danger, and conservatives have long been willing to support large defense budgets, at levels disproportionate to other federal spending, to reduce the likelihood that America might be attacked.

Conservatives also have great respect for the American military, knowing that in the event of war, it is those men and women in uniform who will die on foreign battlefields. One cannot simply wish away the dangers facing us, but neither can one rush into global conflict. In the search for national security, it is true conservatives who offer the best prospect for avoiding future Iraqs. When it comes to war, the true conservative is a centrist: combat is an alternative, but it is the last resort. So long as one of the major political parties, and one of America's major political movements, remains in the grip of people who are neither prudent nor hesitant to embrace war, America will remain on a precipice, always in danger of either failing to act decisively when decisive action is required or leaping too quickly into the maelstrom.

Conservatism matters, too, in a nation that is rapidly undergoing demographic change. The "theocrats" have a vision of the perfect society—how people will act, how they will interact, how they will react. In the previous section, I detailed government's increasing intrusiveness, including its willingness to interfere with private medical decisions and state laws. Many of those diktats from Washington were inspired by a desire to impose conformity with the practices prescribed by certain sectarian beliefs. As observed earlier, Americans tend to be religious, and that can have important and beneficial effects in a nation in which more than three hundred million people live together. Compassion, charity, and love are requisites of a good society, and all are encouraged by each of the great religions of the world. But that is the point—there is not one religion in America, there are many. There are also many Americans, equally citizens, equally protected by the Constitution, who practice no religion at all. Many American liberals proclaim their secularity almost to the point of hostility toward religious practice and the proclamation of religious belief. And many American conservatives insist that ours is a "Christian" nation (sometimes oblivious to the variety of "Christian" beliefs). To let either view dominate the political system is dangerous in a civil, diverse society. Conservatism of the sort embraced during the Goldwater years endorses traditional moral beliefs and practices but insists that such matters are for the individual, not the government, to decide. Whether this view survives the imposition of sectarian prescription or an intolerance for religious practice is critically important to the very nature of the society in which we live.

Finally, many conservatives have attempted to turn the Constitution into a scrap of paper upon which one might scribble any desire, spelling out what constitutes a disturbance of the peace (burning the flag) or the requirements for obtaining a marriage license, as though it were nothing more than a fancy city ordinance. Many liberals have shown similar disdain for what the Constitution says, for example in their desire to ignore the Second Amendment guaranteeing the citizen's right to own a gun. But the Constitution says what it says, and a number of leading liberal supporters of federal gun control, including Professors Laurence Tribe of Harvard, Akhil Reed Amar of Yale, and Sanford Levinson of the University of Texas, have reversed their previous positions and have concluded that the prohibition they support would require a constitutional amendment.

In both cases, the problem is the same—starting with a desired outcome and working backward to find ways to impose that outcome, without concern for what the Constitution allows. There are many valid and serious criticisms of the Constitution as it was originally formulated. In counting population for congressional representation, it treated slaves as partial human beings. It treated women as second-class citizens or worse. And Americans have changed the Constitution to eliminate those national disgraces. But the Constitution was changed to reflect fundamental questions of human liberty, not to prescribe marriage laws or merely impose the public will of the moment. No nation may continue to hold itself out as a "nation of laws" if the law is but shifting sand beneath one's feet.

Why does it matter if American conservatism returns to its principles? If its soul is recaptured? If it is reclaimed from those who have so terribly disfigured it? It matters because liberals too often believe in enhancing the power of the state and are too willing to sacrifice the rights of individuals to the collective, and because to-day's conservatives have adopted the same view. Both seem inclined to envision a perfect society and then to impose it on the rest of us. In the debates to come, America needs one group of men and women whose commitment is to a government that adheres to the Constitution, one that respects the restraints that safeguard the civil, human, constitutional rights of the American people.

A ROADMAP TO THE FUTURE

This is the nexus. During the early years of George W. Bush's presidency, the chief executive became a mini-monarch who decided which laws to obey and which to ignore, and the Constitution's "first branch" of government was transformed into an almost irrelevant extension of the White House staff. And this happened not despite the conservative rise to power but as a direct result of it. Those who ran Congress during the president's grab for power betrayed not only the Constitution but the very political movement they pretended to represent.

Because of a propensity for preservation of the status quo, or at least a well-honed sense of caution in accepting change, conservatives long ago were given the same label applied to European political movements that were resistant to change. But as we've seen, the titles were misleading. When they rallied behind Barry Goldwater, they closely resembled Europe's classical liberals, who placed greater emphasis on individual rights and challenged the centralized authority of nobles and kings. The traditions they sought to conserve were embodied in the Constitution, a flawed but distinctly liberal (that is, pro–individual rights) document. If Democratic presidents had attempted to accrue the unchallenged authority that has been a hallmark of the current Bush presidency, conservatives would have risen up in full-throated opposition.

Whatever their differences, all conservatives believe there is something inherently unique about America. They may disagree sharply over issues such as environmental preservation, the proper amount of public support for the less fortunate, the extent to which religious beliefs ought to influence or be reflected in public policy decisions. But a clear line has separated conservatives from non-conservatives. For most of the past forty years, it has been the line that also separates what government may do from what it may not do. For conservatives, the emphasis has been not on empowerment but on constraint—keeping intact those barriers that keep government action within proper bounds.

Constrained government was, for conservatives, a uniting belief. Others who share my concern about the transformation of the conservative movement focus primarily on the increase in public spending—and public debt—that marked the convergence of a conservative presidency and a conservative Congress. But while opposition to debt and limits on spending were always important for conservatives, the greater concern was for preserving the walls the founders had erected. Conservatism is not a philosophy of green eyeshades and dusty ledgers; it is driven by ideas, the most important of which, the various guarantees of individual rights and civil liberties, are those found within the Constitution. To rail against the erosion of conservative principle because of an increase in the level of government spending is to miss the point entirely. Yes, budget deficits are potentially harmful, and government that grows too large could also be too intrusive, but it is the intrusiveness, beyond the limits of constitutional authority, not the size or cost of government alone, that is the problem. Any member of Congress, talk-show host, blogger, or blowhard who complains about government spending but supports the right of a president to ignore the law, or who would surrender fundamental legislative authority to a chief executive, forfeits any claim to speak on conservatism's behalf.

As do those who have expanded government secrecy, asserted almost unbridled executive authority to disregard the law, misled the people's Congress about the cost and effect of federal programs, ignored treaties approved by the people's elected representatives, sought to overturn or undermine the results of state elections. They have embraced everything that conservatives fought against for decades. It is time for conservatives to reclaim their movement.

This is not just about whether gays marry or protesters burn flags or corporations are called to account. This is about a much more fundamental question: Who decides? It is not a question of specific policy proposals; it is a question of what kind of society we want ours to be. In the last forty years, conservatives have crossed from one side of a line to the other—from the side of limited government and protected freedom to the side of regulation and federal control. We need to go back, and what follows are steps along that road.

Step #1. Remember that we are
a religious people but a secular nation

The brand of conservatism that emerged after George Wallace's followers drifted into the Republican Party and began to reshape the party and its core platform was far removed from the Constitution-based principles that originally lay at the movement's heart. This new, southern, conservatism stressed not individual liberty but social norms—and a willingness to use the federal and state governments to enforce compliance. Where conservatism had been a political and philosophical movement, it began to resemble a social movement, incorporating into its "political" agenda issues from outside the political domain.

A similar focus characterized the Moral Majority and, to an even greater extent, the Christian Coalition. In recent years, many liberals have wondered why voters so often seem to vote against their own interests, by which they generally mean the voter's economic interests. This analysis sees voters as essentially rational actors, calculating advantage and disadvantage. But—and this is a point too often missed by political scientists, many of whom act and think like economists—politics is not essentially a rational (that is, intellectually calculating) activity. Most voters are moved primarily by their instincts: their fears, their aspirations, the environments in which they feel comfortable, and those that make them feel as though the old anchors are being jerked away. Change—especially change in social relationships and the displacement of the traditional—can be a strong motivator for resistance. We all tend to have strong feelings about the kind of society we want to live in and the kind of society we do not want to live in. No appeal to economic advantage is likely to offset prohibitions against prayers in the classroom or Christmas displays on a courthouse lawn.

There is, of course, nothing wrong with working to shape society along certain lines. Religious leaders including Billy Graham and thousands of ministers, priests, rabbis, and imams have used their powers of persuasion to guide social interaction. In the finest community-based self-help tradition, nonprofit organizations and countless individuals have worked to create schools, job training programs, and health care clinics without federal involvement. When Hillary Clinton invoked the African proverb that "it takes a village" to raise a child, she was right, and across America, thousands of "villages" are working to do just that.

Where the line must be drawn, however, is between persuasion and compulsion. The Constitution is for all Americans—Catholic, Protestant, Jewish, Buddhist, Muslim, and nonbeliever alike. We are free to practice or not as we deem fit. Religion is a personal thing; government is what we hold in common, and that distinction lies at the heart of American conservatism. Community is not the same thing as government. The U.S. government is a secular institution, and its policy decisions should not be required to conform to religious doctrine.

George Wallace is long gone from the American political scene. But the kind of intolerant traditionalism he mobilized came to cast a dark shadow over the conservative movement even though it was the polar opposite of the emphasis on individuality that had been at the heart of American conservatism. Pat Robertson, on the other hand, remains a factor in the public discourse. So does the Christian Coalition. And although both Robertson and his organization have every right to their views (despite what some secularists seem to believe, the Constitution does not mandate that people with strong religious convictions stand on the policy sidelines), views that may help shape Republican politics, their guiding light is the degree to which an individual conforms to a collective orthodoxy of religious sectarianism. And that is not American conservatism. The legacies of George Wallace and Pat Robertson are heavy anchors dragging what was once a soaring conservative idealism back to a muddy earth.

Step #2. Reject the destructive legacy
of Newt Gingrich

The nationwide thumping that Republicans received in the 2006 midterm elections was primarily a repudiation of the arrogance and incompetence of the Bush administration, so much so that by the end of the campaign many Republican candidates were doing their best to distance themselves from the president. But it was not entirely ascribable to Bush. Polls also revealed a deep public dissatisfaction with Congress. Much of the blame for that anger can be traced directly back to Gingrich.

By 2006, Gingrich was no longer the Speaker of the House; he was no longer even a member of Congress. Those in charge were Dennis Hastert and Tom DeLay, neither of whom were Gingrich protégés (in fact, both had vigorously opposed Gingrich's rise to leadership). But when they came to power, neither man deviated much from the Gingrich playbook. That is, both saw governance as warfare being waged twenty-four hours a day, 365 days a year. The pursuit of power became the primary governing principle. Earlier

I mentioned that Karl Hess, the Goldwater speechwriter who later became a far-Left activist, sent me a letter in which he had written, "Remember, the enemy is the state." Gingrich, too, saw politics in terms of allies and enemies. To him, the enemy was the Democratic Party, and it was he who transformed the fight for control of Congress from a district-by-district choice between competing candidates to a nationwide no-holds-barred struggle between warring political parties.

Under Gingrich's leadership, conservatives became Republicans first and conservatives second (a factor that eventually led to the strange sight of a "conservative" Congress creating major new spending programs and fueling record deficits). Republicans had long been hungry for a chance to affect policy, and after forty years in the minority wilderness without a single Republican committee or subcommittee chairman in Congress, an institution in which chairmanships convey strategic dominance over entire legislative agendas, they had that chance. What mattered, now that power had been gained, was keeping it—keeping control, even if that meant abandoning the governing philosophy that had guided conservatives for half a century.

There are probably no conservatives currently serving in Congress who can equal Gingrich when it comes to ego; soon after being elected Speaker of the House, he followed President Clinton's State of the Union speech with one of his own even though the Constitution mandates that the president give such a report but somehow failed to ask that a member of Congress give one as well. But though Gingrich's hubris may be singular, his politics-as-warfare, the-other-party-as-enemy credo is not, and it continues to dominate Republican congressional politics. If conservatives want to regain the philosophical high ground they once occupied, they must reject the very basic premises of Gingrich's entire approach to national governance: politics is not, in fact, simply war by another name; politics is politics—a debate about alternatives. If the conservatives who dominate the House Republican membership continue to pursue a policy of winning at any cost, of remaining in campaign mode after the elections have ended and the responsibility for governing has begun, they will betray not only their own principles but any right to lead the country.

The road back lies not merely in a different direction from that charted by Gingrich, but in its polar opposite. For years, conservatives battled to win dominance in the Republican Party at the national, state, and local levels. The idea driving the effort was simple: conservatives would remain united behind their principles (primarily an emphasis on constitutional liberty) and, by gaining control of the Republican Party's managing machinery, use that vehicle to take the movement into the ranks of public decision-makers. Instead of the Republican Party becoming an arm of conservatism, however, the reverse happened. The GOP swallowed the movement.

Political parties are not based on any governing principle. They may at times be dominated by one ideological strain or by a combination of several, but their sole purpose is to win elections. This is especially true in American politics, with its two dominant parties. Many nations put numerous parties on the ballot, each with its own candidates and its own platforms, its own candidates for national leadership, and its own narrowly defined public policy targets. America's leading parties (the only ones that ever stand much of a chance in most elections) are "umbrella" parties, encompassing a wide variety of perspectives. The Republican Party, for example, may include constitutional libertarians, traditionalist and/or religious conservatives, "moderates" (who may have feet planted firmly in several camps simultaneously) and, especially in the Northeast, liberals. The party is not a representative of a particular political point of view; it is, at best, a contained coalition. Some may be in favor of gay rights, some may oppose it. Some may believe in free trade, others in protectionism. Some may want to launch a preemptive, or even a preventive, military strike; others may find the idea appalling. In such a case, what is the responsibility of the party (regardless of what its platform may claim)? To elect every one of the above, for they will strengthen the party's numbers and increase its chances to gain control of the House, or Senate, or state legislature, or city council. Will this necessarily enable the party's members to pass legislation that will enhance the protection of constitutional liberties? No. It will merely give the party an added advantage in seeking the support of even more voters in the next election, so it may elect even more party members, then repeat the cycle all over again.

The party also has another goal: to defeat members of the opposition, no matter what. Gingrich was a specialist at "wedge issues." The tactic was simple—whenever they could get away with it, Republicans under his leadership would force issues to a recorded vote on the House floor, even if it was clear that they had no chance of passing. The sole purpose was to force Democrats to vote in accordance with their own consciences or to reflect the (perhaps transitory) preferences of their constituents. The great British statesman Edmund Burke had argued persuasively that legislators owed it to their constituents to be more than mere rubber stamps for fleeting public opinion, but to bring to bear on each vote they cast their best judgment. Newt Gingrich's aim was to make every Democrat who did so pay a heavy price and to force his fellow Republicans to put their own best judgments on hold in deference to the ongoing battle for partisan advantage.

Gingrich wanted to transform America's legislative system, and the relationship between the executive and the legislative branches, into something resembling the British parliamentary system. But the founders were very familiar with the parliamentary system and its party-versus-party formulation, and they wanted absolutely no part of it. They made that plain in Article 1, Section 6, of the Constitution in which they wrote: "No Person holding any Office under the United States, shall be a Member of either House during his Continuance in Office"—a direct, unmistakable, and very deliberate break from the British system in which the executive is the head of one of the political parties, sits in the legislative chambers, and sets his party's legislative agenda.

This lurch toward a parliamentary system—party above all—had a number of seriously detrimental effects. For one thing, a democracy is supposed to provide an arena in which people of differing opinions—and representing citizens with different opinions—struggle over national policy. Partisanship for its own sake reduces politics to a cynical game of personal advantage. As a result, the public throws up its hands and either turns away from the political process or turns toward demagogues. But politics—the shaping of national priorities—is an honorable undertaking. When it turns citizens into cynics, those who practice it should take a hard look in the mirror. Had conservatives done so during the years of Gingrich's leadership, they might not have liked what they saw.

There was another consequence, one of even greater magnitude. When one's party rather than one's constituency becomes the most important factor, it creates a natural tendency for members of that party to follow the leader. When that leaders sits in the White House, with all the publicity advantages of the presidency, the tendency is even more pronounced and can lead members of Congress to see themselves as subservient to the party member in the Oval Office.

In addition, when party matters most, justifying an unremitting year-round assault on members of an opposing party is easy. Rather than an examination of proposed policy alternatives, it's Jets versus Sharks. Enmity between members of the parties increases the unwillingness to compromise that has so frequently characterized post-Gingrich politics. Instead of the campaign season going on hiatus at the conclusion of an election, the attacks persist, breeding a national cynicism with a very disturbing practical effect: it makes it harder to persuade citizens to vote, much less run for public office.

What does party dominance have to do with conservatism? The answer is, "Nothing." And conservatives should no longer support it. It is time for them to again look at the Republican Party as nothing more than a vehicle through which to advance their beliefs in constrained, Constitution-centered government. When party comes first, principle does not come second; it gets lost altogether.

It is true that given America's political system, conservatives who wish to help set national priorities will have to find a home in one of the two parties. But conservatives should make clear that they don't want to be a part of the game whose rules Gingrich devised. If they are elected as Republicans, they will increase Republican numbers and help Republicans gain committee chairmanships in Congress, state legislatures, city councils, or school boards. But the party will have to pay a price for conservative participation: party leaders will have to understand that conservatives will evaluate each issue through their own independent perspectives. Conservatives should no longer be expected to set aside their principles to protect a partisan majority.

To any conservative focused on compliance with constitutional safeguards, a declaration of independence from the Republican Party will offer a pathway to public service based on principle. And it will permanently erase the corrosive effect of the Gingrich era on both civility and the Constitution.

Step #3. Re-embrace the commitment to "peace through strength"

The Bush administration has weakened the United States and taken the nation into an unnecessary war that has proved to be a disaster. The nation has lost considerable "hard power" (the military is stretched impossibly thin and would be hard-pressed to deal with emerging threats) and "soft power" (its prestige, goodwill, and diplomatic leadership). Professing to be supportive of the military, the administration sent Americans into combat underequipped and with an insufficient number of troops. Its policies embraced neither peace nor strength, and conservatives simply watched with scarcely a protest and almost abject compliance.

I've noted that during FDR's presidency, Harry Truman, a senator of the president's own party, undertook an intensive investigation of the War Department. Who could imagine the conservatives who dominated the Senate for most of the Bush presidency conducting a similar investigation of Donald Rumsfeld's Defense Department?

Conservatives must again become champions of "peace through strength." For "peace" they must again don the mantle of skepticism, offering support for military action only as a last resort and only after the necessity of war has been made clear as a result of a thorough and independent congressional investigation. And they should demand a full accounting of every aspect of the war effort and exert the immense powers of Congress—subpoena power, appropriations power, and investigatory power—to enforce those demands.

As for the "strength" part of the equation, conservatives must again become the champions of America's military forces, pushing for adequate troop levels and equipment. It is the Congress, not the president, that bears the constitutional responsibility to "support" and "maintain" the nation's armed forces.

Step #4. Support rational federal spending limits

Before "cut and run" there was "tax and spend"—repeated in countless speeches and campaign commercials—accusing liberals of having no compunction about creating an ever-increasing number of expensive federal programs and raising taxes to pay for them. For years, liberals had argued that federal deficits didn't really matter because it was money we owed to ourselves. They opposed proposals to reduce marginal tax rates and to eliminate double taxation.

In article after article, conservative commentators railed against liberal profligacy. But that was then.

My own objections to the performance of this president and a compliant Congress have more to do with the ceding, and usurping, of legislative authority, but it is impossible not to recognize that conservatives have, in this way, too, become what they so long opposed. During the Bush presidency and the half-dozen most recent years of conservative control of Congress, the federal deficit mushroomed, and not only because of the wars in Afghanistan and Iraq. How strange it was in 2006 to hear Democrats campaigning against Republican conservatives for their failure to control federal spending.

Fiscal sanity is a main course of the conservative political menu. There will always be temptations to win the support of various voting blocs by creating new federal programs or increasing appropriations for existing programs. There will always be political advantage from incorporating "special favor" earmarks into federal budgets. But conservatism is a philosophy of prudent stewardship; that is what it means to "conserve."

Step #5. Issue a new declaration of independence

In a broad-based democracy, one must often build coalitions or alliances to achieve political ends. The problem comes when the need to maintain the coalition takes on greater importance than the allegiance to the principles that caused one to seek political victory in the first place. You win, yet forget why that victory was important in the first place.

Conservatism is not about victory per se; it's about principle. Each of us has multiple identities; in our public lives, we wear more than one hat. One may be simultaneously a conservative, a Republican (or a conservative Democrat), a person of religious faith (or not), and a member of a variety of other groups. A conservative who seeks to engage in the world of politics, however, accepts a quite specific obligation regardless of which hat he or she is wearing—an obligation to make political determination fit within the framework of the Constitution.

Of course one may belong to a political party and do one's best to elevate that party to a position of governing dominance. In fact, if a person truly believes in his or her political principles, it is logical that that person would strive for party victory at the polls. As a conservative and a Republican, I often supported candidates whose views did not mirror my own, but whose victory, I felt, would further the successful promotion of the policies I supported. But when the pursuit of electoral victory diminishes, rather than enhances, the achievement of goals, it is time to cut loose.

The pursuit of conservative principles has been severely compromised by three superseding allegiances: to president (when the president is of the same political party); to party, and to religious identity. As I've mentioned earlier, whereas American conservatism has a specific purpose, the preservation of the constitutional system and its prohibitions against the denial of "unalienable rights," political parties have no agenda other than to gain power and hold it, and to do so by whatever stratagems will accomplish the purpose. It is time for conservatives to declare their independence: to stand with Republicans, to advance the party's political strength, but not to follow it when it abandons fundamental constitutional principles.

Just as conservatives must reduce their dependency on, and blind allegiance to, a political party, they must reassert their belief in the deliberate constitutional separation of powers. In a time of national security threat, or any other period of great challenge, one hopes for a sufficiently strong president. But the presidency must be kept within bounds, or freedom itself will be at jeopardy. No president should be able to count on loyalty if loyalty implies an unwillingness to perform one's own constitutional obligations or to sit idly by while constitutional limits are cast aside as inconvenient trifles.

Conservatism is a philosophy of government, not one of latching onto the "hero" of the moment.

Finally, conservatives must declare their independence from any other force that would seek to shape their political undertakings. Religion can be a powerful force for good, and the values bred by religion can be praiseworthy. All Americans are free to apply these beliefs in their daily lives. But what is permitted in the interactions between neighbors is quite different from what is permitted in the interactions between citizens and their government. Conservatives must declare independence both from those who advocate policies based on a particular scriptural interpretation and from those who believe religion should be frozen out of public life altogether. We are a collective society with many needs in common, and we have a government properly empowered to function, within limits, on our behalf. But we are also a society that is committed to honoring, respecting, and defending the fundamental rights of each of its citizens. According to the mandate that created this country, this is what we are. This is what we are supposed to be.

Step #6. Rethink the attitude toward government

Ronald Reagan famously declared that "government is not the solution to our problem; government is the problem." To a great many conservatives, that was the movement's philosophy in a nutshell: The enemy is the State.

The problem is, that was neither what Reagan said nor meant. Reagan spent sixteen years in government; Barry Goldwater spent thirty-four years in government, thirty in the United States Senate and four as a member of the Phoenix City Council. Even James Madison, the man who most shaped a nation designed to keep its government under control, spent a sizable portion of his life in government. These were not men who despised government or fled from government service.

What, then, did Reagan mean? To answer that, we need to look at the words themselves, not a bumper sticker abbreviation. *"In the present crisis,"* Reagan said in his inauguration speech, referring to the then-current state of federal affairs, including high taxes and high levels of federal spending, "government is not the solution to our problem; government is the problem." "From time to time," Reagan said, "we've been tempted to believe that society has become too complex to be managed by self-rule, that government by an elite group is superior to government for, by, and of the people." Reagan was not calling for a rejection of government, but for a better management of government, with proper respect for constitutional constraints and for greater, not less, citizen participation. "All of us together, *in* and out of government, must bear the burden." "Now, so there will be no misunderstanding," Reagan continued, "it's not my intention to do away with government. It is rather to make it work—work with us, not over us; to stand by our side, not ride on our back. Government can and must provide opportunity, not smother it; foster productivity, not stifle it."

Of course, government *can* be a problem and often is. It can take away too much in taxes and stifle incentive and production. It can overregulate. It can be too intrusive. It can become bogged down in paper and rules and guidelines that frustrate rather than help. But government is not the problem; the management of government is the problem. Policymakers can be replaced, and the system can be reformed, because ours is not "government" at a distance but that wonderful fulfillment of human aspiration—*self*-government. It is a government in which the people choose their leaders, replace them when they're not meeting expectations, and let them know on a regular basis which policies are, and are not, acceptable.

When Reagan became president in 1981, Democrats had occupied the White House for twelve of the previous twenty years and had controlled Congress for almost three decades. But by the beginning of 2007, conservatives had controlled Congress for ten years and had controlled the White House for twenty-six of the previous thirty-four years. If government was the enemy, who was to blame?

It is time for conservatives to shelve the ludicrous antigovernment chatter that has been dominating their rhetoric for years. This is not the distant government of King George III; our government was voted into office by American citizens under a Constitution that allows them to govern themselves. It is to be celebrated, not trashed. It is restrained, but it has legitimate and important functions to perform, and conservatives should embrace the opportunity to shape the performance of those functions.

Step #7. Reexamine basic values

Those who now call themselves "conservative" have managed to forget whose side they're on. A number of critics have observed that the conservative default position today too often appears to be a knee-jerk defense of any corporate or professional wrongdoing. It sometimes seems that conservatives have switched sides—from protecting the rights of the individual to accepting the idea of capitalism as a devil-take-the-hindmost, law-of-the-jungle, survival-of-the-fittest economic struggle—the opposite of the earlier conservative concern for open competition and equal opportunity.

But there is another area, also, in which conservatives have lost sight of their values. Many Americans today would find it inconceivable that conservatives would consider themselves careful stewards of the environment, yet that is precisely what they were at one time. In *The Conservative Mind* (1953), Russell Kirk wrote, "We live beyond our means by . . . insatiably devouring minerals and forests and the very soil, lowering the water table, to gratify the appetites of the present tenants of the country." Here is his description of the proper conservative attitude: "Turning away from the furious depletion of natural resources, we ought to employ our techniques of efficiency in the interest of posterity, voluntarily conserving our land and our minerals and our forests and our water and our old towns and our countryside for the future partners in our contract of eternal society."

"The modern spectacle of vanished forests and eroded lands, wasted petroleum and ruthless mining . . ." he noted, "is evidence of what an age without veneration does to itself and its successors."

Five years before Kirk's seminal book, Richard Weaver, another of the early conservative intellectuals, wrote, "Man has a duty of veneration toward Nature. . . . Nature is not something to be fought, conquered and changed according to any human whims. . . . What man should seek in regard to nature is not a complete dominion . . . but a decent humility."

It is a betrayal of conservative values to defend excessive exploitation of our natural world. Barry Goldwater gloried in nature, loved the environment, and embraced his beautiful Arizona countryside. He was a tree-hugger. Repeatedly he argued that the principal difference between conservatives and liberals was the liberal propensity for seeing man entirely in economic terms, while conservatives preferred to see man in a more holistic sense, as a being with a soul, a spirit. It is the essential difference between the liberal's insistence on giving a hungry man a fish and a conservative's insistence on also teaching him how to catch more fish. But of course the analogy works only if any fish remain.

Now it is conservatives who increasingly attempt to weigh issues solely by an economic yardstick, applying a cost-benefit analysis to proposals for environmental protection. Weighing cost against benefit is only common sense, of course, but only if one properly considers all the elements of cost. Some costs are not monetary (the costs of lost beauty, for example, or increased risk to health).

There is a value in a clean environment that goes beyond savings in medical bills. There is value in biological diversity that goes beyond keeping fish alive for fishermen. What love do I show a child—what sort of "family value" do I exhibit—when I send him or her off to school through air heavy with pollution or fix school lunches with water that has had to be filtered and refiltered to screen out metals and waste?

Where the founders struggled to guard against any one faction dominating, conservatives now often seem in thrall to one faction over others: Big Business. They should be as opposed to the tyranny of business as to the tyranny of a bureaucracy. Nowhere is this abandonment of conservative principle more obvious than in the absurd notion that a conservative would somehow applaud the destruction of forests and wildlife habitats. In *The Conscience of the Majority*, Goldwater wrote a chapter titled "Saving the Earth," in which he wonders whether we would ever be willing to give up the luxury of toxic pesticides and animal skins. The great conservative thinkers considered humans the stewards of the planet. Many of today's conservatives seem to believe less in maximizing freedom or safeguarding the planet than in maximizing profit. If our children suffer, so be it.

Step #8. Reread the Constitution

I've noted that in old-style monarchies, a king or queen wore two crowns simultaneously: he or she was both the head of state and head of government. A president of the United States is indeed the head of state—the official representative of the nation—but he is not, in fact, the head of government. He is the head of one of three equal branches of government. Remembering this simple fact had long been a centerpiece of conservative policy. In 1966, for example, an editorial in *Rally*, a conservative monthly, declared, "One of the most important . . . reforms is to return to Congress its full independence and legislative authority." An editorial a few months later stated that "the future of the conservative/libertarian enterprise lies overwhelmingly in Congress, rather than the presidency." Conservatives railed against presidents bypassing the regular legislative process by issuing executive orders. Constraints on the concentration of power were seen as the best means of protecting citizens' rights and liberties.

But by the time Reagan became president, conservatives had come to the conclusion that the best way to achieve their goals—a stronger military capability, lower tax rates, smaller government, leaner budgets, less regulation—was to put as much of the nation's decision-making authority as possible in the hands of the only conservative in Washington who appeared to have any real power. Bertolt Brecht had suggested in a poem that perhaps the government could elect a new people. Because conservatives had no such option—they were stuck with the populace that had repeatedly put Democrats (and liberals) in control of Congress—they began a long campaign to strip constitutional authority from the people's branch of government and place as much governmental control as possible in the White House. The Constitution obligated Congress to sign off on international treaties, but conservatives supported legislation to strip Congress of the right to amend treaties that the White House negotiated. The Constitution charges Congress with setting budget levels and spending priorities, but conservatives supported legislation transferring de facto control over spending to the president. After decades of leading the opposition to centralized authority, conservatives became its champions.

If conservatives are to reclaim any semblance of their original principles, the road back begins with the Constitution itself.

Article 1, Section 1: "All legislative Powers herein granted shall be vested in a Congress of the United States, which shall consist of a Senate and House of Representatives."

The Constitution states, quite clearly, that *all* legislative authority, not merely authority over domestic issues, is vested in Congress. It does not provide for a Congress that is to serve in an advisory capacity to the president, or for members of the president's party to serve as his legislative assistants. It does not say that some legislative power resides in Congress and the rest with the president.

There have been numerous federal court cases holding that Congress's power to legislate includes the power to conduct inquiries and investigations. There have also been numerous federal court cases confirming that Congress has the power to punish for contempt in the course of its investigations.

It is Congress—not the president, and not the federal departments or agencies—in which the Constitution places the responsibility for determining the law and for conducting the oversight hearings and investigations to ensure that the laws are being followed and that the executive branch is neither ignoring the law nor abusing its authority. It is the job of conservatives to insist on aggressive oversight of the White House and of government agencies, and that is true even if a member of their party sits in the White House. That is part of a member of Congress's legislative obligation; it is also part of conservatism's fundamental political belief system.

Article 1, Section 2: "The House of Representatives shall chuse their Speaker." . . . "The Senate shall chuse their other Officers" ("other" meaning other than the president of the Senate, an office held by the Vice president of the United States).

Nothing was more abhorrent to any conservative sense of constrained government than the acquiescence of Republican senators to President Bush's involvement in installing Tennessee Senator Bill Frist as Senate majority leader. As it happens, Frist was a colossal flop in the position, understanding neither his own role nor the Senate's in the constitutional framework. But even if he had proved to be adept, both as a senator and as a leader, no conservative should have voted for him to assume a leadership position after the president urged his selection. It was an egregious betrayal of the system of division between the branches of government and a major step toward consolidation, not constraint, of federal power.

Article 1, Section 7: "All Bills for raising Revenue shall originate in the House of Representatives . . ."

Nowhere is the intent of the framers more clearly represented than in this provision. In the early days of the Republic—and for more than a decade into the twentieth century—senators were elected not by the public at large but by members of the various state legislatures. Presidents were elected by the nation as a whole. This provision of the Constitution makes plain that if the people are to be taxed, the level of taxation should be determined by that branch of the government that is closest to them, the House of Representatives. During the Bush presidency, it was characteristic of the Republican Congress to merely rally behind tax legislation proposed by the White House, giving the president the tax package he requested, minus whatever small changes were ultimately forced upon it by opponents. Whether or not one agrees with the direction of a president's tax policy is beside the point; the proper position for any conservative member of Congress is to take the proposal under consideration and to evaluate its likely effects on the various segments of society and its influence on the overall health of the economy. To serve as presidential "cheerleaders" is demeaning to both Congress (and its members) and the Constitution.

Article 1, Section 7: "Every Bill which shall have passed the House of Representatives and the Senate, shall, before it become a Law, be presented to the president of the United States; if he approve he shall sign it, but if not he shall return it, with his Objections to that House in which it shall have originated, who shall enter the Objections at large on their Journal, and proceed to reconsider it. If after such Reconsideration two thirds of that House shall agree to pass the Bill, it shall be sent, together with the Objections, to the other House, by which it shall likewise be reconsidered, and if approved by two thirds of that House, it shall become a Law."

When a president is presented with a piece of legislation, he has two choices: sign it or veto it. If there is a clear division between the role of the president and the role of Congress, this is it. Congress writes the laws; the president need not go along—he can pressure Congress to change its mind or rally the congressional votes to sustain his veto—but he may not "amend" the law by picking and choosing which pieces to obey. And he may not refuse to obey the law, as Bush has tried to do through the use of the "signing statements" described at the beginning of this book.

Every member of Congress, Republican or Democrat, conservative or liberal, should be forced by his or her constituents to demand that any president, regardless of party, follow the Constitution and abide by any statute that has been signed into law. No exceptions. No silence. Here lies the line between constitutional government and unchecked power.

Article 1, Section 8: "The Congress shall have Power" to
  "lay and collect taxes";
  "provide for the common Defence";
  "borrow Money on the credit of the United States";
  "regulate Commerce with foreign Nations";
  "declare War";
  "make Rules concerning Captures on Land and Water";
  "raise and support Armies";
  "provide and maintain a Navy";
  "make Rules for the Government and Regulation of the land and naval forces";
  "provide for calling forth the Militia";
  "provide for organizing, arming, and disciplining, the Militia, and for governing such Part of them as may be employed in the Service of the United States";

"make all Laws which shall be necessary and proper for carrying into Execution the foregoing Powers, and all other Powers vested by this Constitution in the Government of the United States."

Here is the proper question for any conservative to ask of anybody who would be president or serve as a member of Congress: "What part of this do you *not* understand?"

Congress, not the president, has the responsibility for taxation. Yet the pattern has become to use the president's tax proposals as the legislative starting point, turning the Constitution on its head.

As most Americans now realize, the Republican Congress's greatest failure, and its most radical departure from conservative principles, was in failing to scrutinize President Bush's determination to go to war in Iraq. It bears repeating: the conservative approach to war is based on caution, prudence, a search for ways to keep the peace. Congress is constitutionally charged with the responsibility—and sole authority—to decide whether the United States should go to war; and Congress, not the president, has sole authority under the Constitution to decide what to do about captured enemy combatants. In addition, decisions about arming and disciplining and governing the actions of members of the National Guard are congressional decisions, not presidential decisions.

The founders deliberately withheld these powers from the president. They go to the heart of the Constitution, and they are to rest with the people, not an imperial "decider-in-chief." Restraint of power and the division of authority are at the core not only of America but of American conservatism.

A FINAL WORD

For more than forty years I have devoted myself to the classical liberal tradition which has become known in the United States as conservatism—"conservative" because it is dedicated to the preservation of the fundamental principles of the American Constitution—and unconvinced that a departure from those principles is somehow "progressive." In fact, centralized direction is not "progressive" at all; it is the oldest system of governance known to man, practiced by kings, warlords, and cave dwellers. What *is* progressive is a system in which the main duty of the governors is to protect the rights of the people. That is the unique creation of America's founders. Throughout my political life, that was the principle that lay at the heart of American conservatism, too.

True conservatives were never antigovernment; they were for a clear delineation between where government authority ended and individual rights began. They were for government that was accountable and that performed its functions well. They were for government that was prudent, frugal, honest, and civil. Today, all of those important goals have been compromised. Conservatives have undermined the central feature of the Constitution, the separation of powers; have signed off on policies that should have been challenged more forcefully; have spent taxpayers' dollars and increased the public's debt at rates that liberals can only marvel at; have presided over a cycle of nastiness that has undermined public confidence in our government institutions; and have acted too slowly to probe allegations of wrongdoing.

Today, commentators are quick to criticize the "earmarking" of federal spending. But of course it is Congress, not the executive branch, that is supposed to make spending determinations. It is appropriate for Congress to earmark—that is, to decide how much money will be spent where. The problem is not earmarks but the ways in which those earmarks were incorporated into congressional appropriations—secretly, anonymously, and without debate. How can that cavalier use of the taxpayers' money be squared with a philosophy which has always held that government was to be watched, scrutinized, checked, and kept answerable to the people?

Here's a plea: from time to time, public officials go off on retreats at which they discuss various aspects of their work. Perhaps it is time for conservatives, and especially those in Congress, those who have actively or passively participated in the erosion of the constitutional system, to go off not in groups, but by themselves. To take a few days for self-reflection. To ask themselves what is required of men and women who enter public service. And to reacquaint themselves with what it means to truly be a conservative—a distinctly American conservative.

For nearly eight years now, American public policy has been shaped, in whole or in part, by a president of the United States who has methodically, unrelentingly, sometimes aggressively and sometimes deceitfully, attempted to replace America's system of decentralized shared-power government with his own vision of a society governed by the few, the powerful, and the increasingly unaccountable.

George W. Bush, whether consciously or not, has viewed the Constitution as outdated, unsuited for the dangers of the modern world, and not designed for the quality of leadership that he felt he had to offer. He may have been derided for his bold assertions that he alone was "the decider," the ultimate decision-maker in American government, but he has never wavered in that belief. It is a legacy that American voters must confront in determining who will hold that office for the next four or eight years.

America will choose a new president in 2008 as well as determine who will sit in Congress. Voters must protect against not only another overreaching, power-grabbing, Constitution-ignoring president—one of those a century is quite enough—but against the sort of acquiescent, duty-ignoring, party-first legislators whose own ignorance of, or lack of respect for, the Constitution is equally as great a threat to American government.

However, it would be a mistake to believe that given what America has endured under the Bush presidency and the extent to which his power grab was abetted by a compliant Republican-dominated Congress, it follows that the solution is to elect a Democratic president and a Congress controlled by Democrats. Democrats are quite as capable as Republicans are of treating the Constitution disrespectfully, and they are no less given to making decisions on the basis of partisan advantage.

It would also be a mistake, or at least an overstatement, to believe that Bush and the Republicans who controlled Congress were solely to blame for the damage done to the Constitution during that period. Many conservative newspaper columnists, talk-show hosts, and issue activists have also long since forgotten what it means to be a conservative. Too many reporters have become accustomed to discussing important national issues in terms of the conflicts that rage around them rather than the principles that underlie them. The national news media generally finds it easier to focus its reporting on the pronouncements and machinations of a few individuals in the White House rather than on the clumsy, messy, and often uncoordinated struggles that take place within Congress (a singular mark of democracy). Educators in even the most prestigious university government departments (including the Kennedy School of Government) tend to focus their teaching and their attention on the presidency and the executive branch of government and on issues of government "efficiency"; there are relatively few courses on Congress, the Constitution, or politics, though those form the core of America's democratic system. Indeed, there are many targets at which one may point a finger of blame for the precarious position in which the Constitution now finds itself.

Nonetheless, this book is not an equal-opportunity blamer. I am not a working journalist (though I have been) or a talk-show host or, any longer, a movement activist. I also don't blame liberals; they have never been dishonest about their conviction that government should be used to carry out their social views. Some liberals have dismissed the Constitution as merely an outdated relic written by long-dead, wealthy white men who inhabited a distant and very different age. And the desire to redesign society in what one perceives to be "a better way" is not uncommon to human nature. Rather, it is the conservatives who have said, or used to say, "Hold on, where is the line beyond which government may not step? Where are the liberties that must be protected whether against the few or the many?"

There are many things in the original Constitution that do not fit our modern age. Many have already been addressed, in the Fourteenth Amendment and the Nineteenth Amendment, for example. For those who believe further change is needed, there is a process within the Constitution itself for its revision. James Madison introduced amendments to it, and Thomas Jefferson often spoke of the right of the people to change the nation's governing structure when they thought change necessary. But the changes should be few (the Constitution does not exist to serve as a national equivalent of local city ordinances defining, for example, marriage) and should be undertaken solely in accordance with established legal process, not by an intentional disregard of constitutional provisions. Those limitations are the only way to ensure that we as a people will be governed, and protected in our liberties, by a common national understanding of the law. That, not a childish belief that the founders were infallible, is what lay at the heart of American conservatism. The Constitution, with its constraints on government and its protections for human liberties, was not to be taken lightly, not to be set aside whenever doing so might provide partisan advantage or victory on some issue that seemed important in the moment.

This is why the finger of blame should be pointed directly at those people who call themselves "conservatives." If the Constitution and its fervent embrace of citizen rights is lost, they will bear the responsibility for its demise.

Every generation has its challenges and its moments. Preserving the Constitution is our challenge. And this is our moment.

ACKNOWLEDGMENTS

If you think you can list everybody you're indebted to—everybody who has shaped your thinking, encouraged you, inspired you, and helped you along the way—you're fooling yourself. It can't be done. We're all products of too many inputs to narrow them sufficiently to fit within the space allotted here. So to all those whose names should be included here but are not, I apologize.

My grandparents made the difficult decision to leave their homes and families in eastern Europe and to come to the United States where they and their children could escape persecution and find new opportunities. I never knew my grandparents—they worked hard and died young—but the gift they gave me, the incredible privilege of living in America, is beyond measure and beyond repayment. Robert Frost wrote of a fork in the road; the choice to take one rather than the other "made all the difference." And so it has been for me.

I owe a similar debt to my parents. Growing up without resources neither deterred them nor embittered them. Childhood in
an orphanage did not dampen my father's dynamism or his en-
thusiastic embrace of life. Working two jobs, rising early and coming home late, and working into her seventies did not diminish my
mother's great reservoir of inner strength. My father died while still
in his forties; neither he nor my mother ever set foot in a university
classroom, and yet if I live to be one hundred I will never be their
equal.

Outside my circle of family and friends, I owe debts to a great
many men and women whose words and ideas have greatly influenced my thinking. There are the obvious ones—Locke, Madison,
Emerson—and some perhaps not so obvious: Edna St. Vincent
Millay, in *Renascence*, wrote these words: "*A man was starving in
Capri/ He moved his eyes and looked at me/ I felt his gaze, I heard his
moan/ And knew his hunger as my own.*" Such words burrow deep
inside of you and become a part of who you are. Bernard Crick, in
his book *In Defence of Politics*, wrote, "*Politics is the way a free people
govern themselves.*" Those words, too, have made their mark because
they make clear what obligation we each carry to help shape the
society we live in.

The people of Oklahoma gave me the opportunity to represent
them in Congress for sixteen years; their support and encourage-
ment can never be repaid.

I also owe thanks to several people who have, in one way or
another, given me the further opportunity to engage in the public
discussion. Although I became a regular political columnist for the
Chicago Tribune and *Los Angeles Times*, and wrote frequently for the
Boston Globe and other major newspapers, it was Shelley Cohen of
the *Boston Herald* who first gave me the opportunity to write a
weekly column and thus opened that exciting door for me. Ellen
Weiss, before she moved up the executive ladder, was the editor for
my weekly commentaries on National Public Radio's *All Things
Considered*. Albert Carnesale offered me a teaching position at

Harvard's Kennedy School of Government, where I remained on the faculty for eleven years. Anne-Marie Slaughter brought me to the Woodrow Wilson School at Princeton, where I teach today. Judy Feder provided me with a visiting professorship at Georgetown's Public Policy Institute. I am indebted to each of them.

It was Stan Evans, then the editor of the *Indianapolis News* and national chairman of the American Conservative Union, who first invited me to join ACU's board, from which position I observed much of the unfolding growth of the conservative movement and where I also witnessed, as Stan's successor, the increasing tension between Goldwater conservatives and social-movement activists who saw an embrace of "values" as a good direct-mail fund-raising tool. Although I had already been involved in conservative politics, my years at the ACU gave me a marvelous front-row seat for the transformation discussed in this book.

Because they share my concern about the nastiness and partisanship that have become such a disturbing part of the American political scene, Walter Isaacson, the president of the Aspen Institute, and Bill Budinger, of the Rodel Foundations, have given me a wonderful opportunity to work with the best and the brightest of America's young political leadership—a truly rewarding experience.

I have had a great deal of help in preparing this book. Sadly, all of the mistakes in it are my own, but the parts that are not flawed owe much to a number of people.

Adam Cooke spent an enormous amount of time helping me work through every Republican national convention platform since 1964 to document how that statement of beliefs has changed over time.

At Princeton, I drew not only from the Wilson School's conference on American conservatism, which I co-chaired, but also from conversations over lunch with presidential scholar Fred Greenstein and Chris Eisgruber, the university's provost, who were generous with their time and gave me much to think about. Even though he was deep into writing his own next book, Sean Wilentz of the history department was a great help and pointed out a number of areas that needed additional thought (and, sometimes, revision). Bob Gallucci, the dean of the school of foreign service at Georgetown, also took time to meet with me and I appreciate his input as well.

I am on the board of directors of The Constitution Project and its president, Virginia Sloan, has brought me into contact with a number of other people, conservatives and liberals alike, who share my concern about the drift away from constitutional principles. I have learned from them all.

With any project like this, one invariably calls on any number of people for help in ways great and small. For their willingness to answer my many questions, serve as sounding boards, goad me into rethinking certain conclusions (even when they did not know they were doing so), check my work for accuracy or clarity, or provide important research help, I am grateful to Ken Adelman, Laura Brod, Deb Carstens, Lucy Crawford, Ed Feulner, Lou Fisher, Sharon Bradford Franklin, Leslie Gimbel, three Goldwaters (Joanne, C. C., and Barry Jr.), Susan Eisenhower, Dave Keene, Marty Linsky, and Ginny Sloan.

My assistants—Gia Regan at the Aspen Institute and Bernadette Yeager at Princeton—were of invaluable help to me in keeping my real work on track while I undertook this project. It would be impossible to thank them enough.

I have lucked out as an author in two particularly important ways. I have the world's best agent. For years, Ike Williams kept prodding me to write the book you now hold in your hands. And when I did, he spent hours working with me, helping me shape it into something that might interest a publishing house. Without Ike and his terrific assistant, Hope Denekamp, this book would not have happened. And, since I was on a roll, I also ended up with the world's best editor. For the last several years I have done a great deal of public speaking and somewhat less writing. I had fallen into the speaker's habit of repeating for emphasis; Tim Bent eventually convinced me (though it was hard to do) that less is more and while I do continue to underline by repetition, I do it much less here than in the original draft. If this book reads smoothly, that's Tim's doing.

I have also lucked out in a way that has nothing to do with this book. My wife is Elizabeth Sherman. She did not take my name and she hasn't adopted my political views either. Elizabeth is intimidatingly smart, with an undergraduate degree in political science, a master's in urban policy, and a doctorate in sociology. And she is very political. She is a Democrat and a liberal and my political sparring partner. She keeps me sharp because when it comes to anything political, I can't let my guard down for a minute. Besides which, we love each other. This book is for her.

NOTES

I

A transcript of the House Judiciary Committee hearing can be found at http://judiciary.house.gov/Oversight.aspx?ID=267.

A good starting point for reading about presidential signing statements is Phillip J. Cooper, *By Order of the President: The Use and Abuse of Executive Direct Action* (Lawrence: University Press of Kansas, 2002). See also Cooper's more recent article, "George W. Bush and Edgar Allan Poe and the Use and Abuse of Presidential Signing Statements," *Presidential Studies Quarterly* 35:3 (2005): 515–532.

The GAO findings were published on June 18, 2007, and can be located at http://www.gao.gov.

Barry Goldwater's *The Conscience of a Conservative*, first published by Victor Press in 1960, has been reissued several times, most recently in an edition edited by Goldwater's granddaughter, C. C. Goldwater, and published by Princeton University Press in 2007.

In 1963, the Young Republican National Federation permitted membership until the age of forty. Consequently, many of the YRs who took part in the organization's national convention in San Francisco that year were actually seasoned political activists; many had been elected to public office or were leaders of their state and local party organizations. The election of Donald Lukens, a Goldwater supporter, to the YR chairmanship, against fierce opposition, amounted to an early shot in the battle for party control. As chairman of the Oklahoma YRs I had been selected to serve as the nominal chairman of Lukens's campaign, though my input into the decision-making process was admittedly minimal.

As a part of their focus on Soviet expansionism and on the loss of personal freedom that followed in its wake, conservatives placed great emphasis on the plight of the "captive nations"—countries that had been swept into the Soviet orbit after World War II. I marched outside the Soviet embassy in Washington to protest the occupation of Poland, Lithuania, Latvia, Estonia, and other nations that had found themselves locked behind an "Iron Curtain." In 1959, President Eisenhower declared a "captive nations week" and it has been observed ever since, even outlasting the Soviet Union itself. In June 2007, President Bush attended the unveiling of the Victims of Communism Memorial in Washington, the result of a long effort spearheaded by the Heritage Foundation's Lee Edwards. The memorial grew out of the creation of a National Captive Nations Committee, which had been authorized by Congress and signed into law by President Clinton.

Other conservative voices were heard in the days leading up to Goldwater's emergence, including those of Henry Hazlitt, Leonard

Read, Frank Chodorov, Stefan Possony, M. Stanton Evans, Willmoore Kendall, Peter Viereck, Richard Weaver, and Albert Jay Nock, but they did not equal either the reach or the influence of the commentary emanating from the political left.

Kolbe, Gunderson, and Bauman were not the only gay politicians who contributed significantly to the growth of conservative influence. Terry Dolan, the founder of the National Conservative Political Action Committee (NCPAC), which unfortunately played a large role in the development of modern "social issue" conservatism, and Arthur Finkelstein, a conservative pollster (and the pollster for my early campaigns), were also gay. It is a shame that so few of today's conservative activists recognize the debt they, and their political movement, owe to their gay fellow conservatives.

In regard to Peter Witonski's volumes about the roots of conservative thought, which I dismiss as something quite different from the rights-centered tradition in America, a number of well-known scholars credit Locke with much less influence on the founders than I am inclined to give him. The works of Bernard Bailyn and Gordon Wood are particularly noteworthy. For more on America's Lockean influence, see especially Louis Hartz, *The Liberal Tradition in America: An Interpretation of American Political Thought Since the Revolution* (New York: Harcourt Brace, 1955). Witonski's work is *The Wisdom of Conservatism* (New Rochelle, NY: Arlington House, 1971).

For an overview of post–World War II American society and politics, see James T. Patterson's *Grand Expectations: The United States, 1945–1974* (New York: Oxford University Press, 1996). There were clearly intimations in the 1950s of the upheavals to come but my point is that for most Americans the very real concerns that led to such change in the '60s had not yet come fully into focus.

No single work can fully capture the early years of modern conservatism and its many intellectual strands and personalities. In the list of suggested readings I call attention to several but one place to start is Robert Alan Goldberg's *Barry Goldwater* (New Haven, CT: Yale University Press, 1995). One should also read Friedrich Hayek's *The Road to Serfdom* (Chicago: University of Chicago Press, 1994). The *Time* Magazine article "Box Score for '64," which gives Goldwater the best shot at defeating John F. Kennedy, is available at http://www.time.com.

On the Southern influence within the Republican Party, see Lewis L. Gould's comprehensive *Grand Old Party: A History of the Republicans* (New York: Random House, 2003). For more on Ronald Reagan, see in particular Lou Cannon's *President Reagan: The Role of a Lifetime* (New York: Public Affairs, 2000). For some good overviews of the rise of the conservative movement and its transformation, see Jonathan Schoenwald's *A Time for Choosing: The Rise of Modern American Conservatism* (New York: Oxford University Press, 2001), William Martin's *With God on Our Side: The Rise of the Religious Right in America* (New York: Broadway, 1996), and Lee Edwards's *The Power of Ideas: The Heritage Foundation at 25 Years* (Ottawa, IL: Jameson, 1997).

This book draws heavily on the national platforms adopted by the Republican Party at its quadrennial conventions from 1964 to 2004. Those can be accessed at http://www.presidency.ucsb.edu/platforms.php.

II

The Court of Appeals language citing the Printz ruling can be found in *Lamont v. O'Neill* (285 F3d 9 [2002]).

Because so many public officials are inclined to focus more on outcome than on process, it is not uncommon for "constitutional technicalities" to be brushed aside. In the case of Congress's "interference" with administration support for the Contras, however, the issue was not only a preoccupation with outcome but the fact that so many Americans, including members of Congress, have somehow come to believe that the making of foreign policy is the exclusive domain of the executive branch. Republican Senator Arthur Vandenberg famously cautioned that politics should end "at the water's edge," meaning that the United States should present a united front to the outside world in terms of American foreign policy. But that is not the same as saying that Congress is obligated to support whatever policy is devised by the president. During the debate over aid to the Contras, however, many conservatives seemed to truly believe that because presidents were responsible for negotiation with other governments and had the authority to command American troops in wartime, they had sole dominion over America's involvement in the international arena. It is a view that can be supported only by disregarding the considerable language of the Constitution itself. On the growth of executive power in foreign affairs, see Louis Fisher, *Presidential War Power*, 2nd ed. (Lawrence: University Press of Kansas, 2004).

The campaign for the line-item veto became a test of conservatives' commitment to reduced federal spending. To this day, there are continuing attempts to find ways around the Supreme Court's unambiguous declaration that transferring power over federal spending to the president is unconstitutional. A better solution to the conservatives' dilemma would have been to win sufficient public support to gain control of Congress, but when that happened, they continued to try to divest Congress—and themselves—of control over spending decisions. Nothing better illustrates the degree to which the Constitution has ceased to matter in the attempt to achieve a preferred outcome. The Supreme Court's decision striking down the line-item veto is at *Clinton v. City of New York* (524 U.S. 417, 118 S. Ct. 2091 [1998]).

Although Newt Gingrich and Tom DeLay have been blamed for the partisan management of the House of Representatives—preventing Democrats from offering amendments to legislation, for example— they did not begin the practice nor did it end when Republicans lost control of Congress after the 2004 elections. Some articles have even credited Gingrich with attempts to strengthen the legislative branch in relation to the presidency. Gingrich's contribution to the partisan nastiness that has pervaded American politics since his ascent has centered on three practices in particular: the use of wedge issues offered as legislative alternatives solely for the purpose of weakening Democratic incumbents, turning congressional elections into nation-wide contests between competing parties in a nonstop year-round battle for dominance, and pressuring Republican members of Congress to put money into a common campaign fund in order to be considered for leadership positions in the party and in Congress.

Congress's abandonment of oversight during the years of Republican dominance is described in Elizabeth Williamson's *Washington Post* article, "Revival of Oversight Role Sought," which appeared on April 25, 2007. The partisan focus of the Republican Congress is described in a *Washington Post* article, "Hastert's Team Mentality to Be Tested as Foley Scandal Unfolds," published on October 16, 2006.

James Madison's warnings about the dangers of factions are well worth reading. One source is Clinton Rossiter, ed., *The Federalist Papers* (New York: Penguin, 1999). A sympathetic view of the "unitary executive" is found in Christopher Yoo, Steven Calabresi, and Anthony Colangelo, "The Unitary Executive in the Modern Era, 1945–2004," *Iowa Law Review* 90 (January 2005): 601–731. See also Elizabeth Drew, "Power Grab," in the *New York Review of Books* 53 (June 22, 2006).

Richard Neustadt's book on presidential power, originally published in 1960, was revised and reissued in 1990 as *Presidential Power and the*

Modern Presidents: The Politics of Leadership from Roosevelt to Reagan (New York: Free Press).

III

In the section about Judge Bork I write that advocates of "strict construction" and "originalism" prefer to interpret the Constitution by reference to the intentions of the founders. That is my preferred view, too, but a number of scholars argue that deciphering the founders' intentions is not always an easy task. Here Jack Rakove's excellent book *Original Meanings: Politics and Ideas in the Making of the Constitution* (New York: Knopf, 1996) is well worth considering.

Some would argue that intervention is justified if a nation allies itself ideologically with a potential enemy of the United States (e.g., the Marxist government in Grenada during the 1980s) or if its economic policies pose a threat to American business interests (Venezuela under Hugo Chavez). But unless American security is threatened, militarily or by the loss of vital resources, merely the fact that a nation has a government that is problematic for U.S. policymakers is not sufficient grounds for this country to throw its considerable weight around. The comedian Chevy Chase accurately, if accidentally, summed up the proper conservative view when he portrayed President George H. W. Bush saying, "Wouldn't be prudent." A hallmark of American conservatism is a philosophy of "live and let live" and that applies internationally as well.

The Supreme Court decision in *Hamdan v. Rumsfeld* is at 126 S. Ct. 2749, handed down on June 29, 2006.

Judge Bork's pronouncements can be found in several books, notably *The Tempting of America: The Political Seduction of the Law* (New York:

Free Press, 1990) and *Coercing Virtue: The Worldwide Rule of Judges* (Washington, DC: American Enterprise Institute, 2003).

Information on the work of The Innocence Project can be accessed at http://www.innocenceproject.org.

Zenger's trial is recounted in *John Peter Zenger: His Press, His Trial and a Bibliography of Zenger Imprints*, published in 1904 by Livingston Rutherfurd (New York: Dodd, Mead). In 2006, Gail Jarrow published an account of the Zenger case for young readers: *The Printer's Trial: The Case of John Peter Zenger and the Fight for a Free Press* (Honesdale, PA: Calkins Creek). Hiller Zobel's *The Boston Massacre* (New York: W. W. Norton, 1970) recounts Adams's defense of the British soldiers accused of murdering five colonists. The Alien and Sedition Acts are examined in James Morton Smith's *Freedom's Fetters: The Alien and Sedition Laws and American Civil Liberties* (Ithaca, NY: Cornell University Press, 1963). Roger Daniels's *Prisoners without Trial: Japanese Americans in World War II* (New York: Hill and Wang, 1993) describes the internments that led to an official apology by Congress and at least a minimal attempt at restitution.

I strongly recommend Fareed Zakaria's *The Future of Freedom: Illiberal Democracy at Home and Abroad* (New York: W. W. Norton, 2003). I wish President George W. Bush had read it.

Joseph S. Nye Jr.'s *Soft Power: The Means to Success in World Politics* (New York: Public Affairs, 2004) examines America's many non-military foreign policy advantages. Despite its title, it is a praise of American muscularity, not weakness.

IV

Many modern conservatives have taken Ronald Reagan's observation that "government *is* the problem" to heart. As is obvious from reading the entire statement, rather than taking it out of context, that is not at all what he meant or what he said. It is frustrating, as a conservative, to hear liberals, whether deliberately or mistakenly, consistently misstate our beliefs. But it is doubly frustrating to recognize that so many conservatives are clueless when it comes to the views of their own alleged heros. Whether it is about championing a government that provides opportunity and fosters productivity (Reagan) or one that works to save the environment and accept individual differences (Goldwater), conservative principles are very different from what many of today's conservatives believe they are. Yes, conservative values have been trashed, but it's conservatives, not liberals, who have been the greatest despoilers of those values.

John Bliese has examined conservatism's perspectives on environmental protection in "Richard M. Weaver, Russell Kirk, and the Environment," *Modern Age* 38 (Winter 1996): 148–158.

For more on Congress's powers to investigate and to punish for contempt, see *Quinn v. United States* (349 U.S. 155, 75 S. Ct. 668 [1955]).

Because so much of the argument in this book relies on the words of the Constitution itself, it is important to emphasize that liberals are right when they say that the Constitution is a *living* document. We do not live in the eighteenth century. But two points must be made: first, the essential nature of the guarantees of the Constitution—the guarantees of civil liberty, or human rights—and the constraints on government that allow those liberties to be preserved are timeless and essential values. They are what makes America America.

SUGGESTED READING

Some of these works present viewpoints similar to my own; others diverge sharply from the perspectives I present in this book. Nonetheless, they are all worth reading. Some have merely served to inform my thinking in a more general way; I present them as books you can learn from, and may be influenced by, whether you agree with them or not. Some flesh out the history—the conflicts, the personalities, and the events—of American conservatism in far greater detail than I was able to do, or wanted to do, in the space of these pages. This is not a bibliography in the sense of being those books on which I built my argument; their influence has been broader than that and over a greater period of time. Nonetheless, if I thought the works listed here would not benefit those who want to think more deeply about the issues I have raised in this book, I would not have listed them.

Martin Anderson. *Revolution*. San Diego: Harcourt Brace Jovanovich, 1988.

Timothy Garton Ash. *Free World: America, Europe, and the Surprising Future of the West*. New York: Random House, 2004.

Randy E. Barnett. *Restoring the Lost Constitution: The Presumption of Liberty*. Princeton: Princeton University Press, 2004.

Alan Barth. *The Rights of Free Men: An Essential Guide to Civil Liberties*. New York: Knopf, 1983.

David Boaz, ed. *The Libertarian Reader: Classic and Contemporary Readings from Lao-tzu to Milton Friedman*. New York: Free Press, 1997.

Derek Bok. *The State of the Nation: Government and the Quest for a Better Society*. Cambridge, MA: Harvard University Press, 1996.

William F. Buckley Jr. *Up from Liberalism*. Rowman and Littlefield, 1961.

James MacGregor Burns. *The Workshop of Democracy*. New York: Knopf, 1985.

George W. Carey, ed. *Freedom and Virtue: The Conservative/Libertarian Debate*. Wilmington, DE: Intercollegiate Studies Institute, 1998.

Stephen L. Carter. *The Dissent of the Governed: A Meditation on Law, Religion, and Loyalty*. Cambridge, MA: Harvard University Press, 1998.

John Chamberlain. *The Roots of Capitalism*. Princeton, NJ: Van Nostrand, 1965.

Phillip J. Cooper. *By Order of the President: The Use and Abuse of Executive Direct Action*. Lawrence: University Press of Kansas, 2002.

Richard C. Cornuelle. *Reclaiming the American Dream*. New York: Random House, 1965.

Alan Crawford. *Thunder on the Right: The "New Right" and the Politics of Resentment*. New York: Pantheon, 1980.

John W. Dean. *Conservatives without Conscience*. New York: Viking, 2006.

Alan M. Dershowitz. *Rights from Wrongs*. New York: Basic Books, 2005.

John J. Dinan. *Keeping the Peoples' Liberties: Legislators, Citizens, and Judges as Guardians of Rights.* Lawrence: University Press of Kansas, 1998.

Elizabeth Drew. *Showdown: The Struggle between the Gingrich Congress and the Clinton White House.* New York: Simon & Schuster, 1996.

Alan O. Ebenstein. *Friedrich Hayek: A Biography.* New York: Palgrave, 2001.

Lee Edwards. *The Conservative Revolution: The Movement That Remade America.* New York: Free Press, 1999.

Lee Edwards. *Goldwater: The Man Who Made a Revolution.* Washington, DC: Regnery, 1995.

Lee Edwards. *The Power of Ideas: The Heritage Foundation at 25 Years.* Ottawa, IL: Jameson, 1997.

Joseph J. Ellis. *Founding Brothers: The Revolutionary Generation.* New York: Knopf, 2000.

Joseph J. Ellis. *His Excellency: George Washington.* New York: Knopf, 2004.

Jean Bethke Elshtain. *Democracy on Trial.* New York: Basic Books, 1995.

M. Stanton Evans. *Revolt on the Campus.* Westport, CT: Greenwood, 1979.

M. Stanton Evans. *Clear and Present Dangers: A Conservative View of America's Government.* New York: Harcourt Brace Jovanovich, 1975.

M. Stanton Evans. *The Future of Conservatism, from Taft to Reagan and Beyond.* New York: Holt, Rinehart and Winston, 1968.

Louis Fisher. *Presidential War Power.* 2nd ed. Lawrence: University Press of Kansas, 2004.

Frances FitzGerald. *Way Out There in the Blue: Reagan, Star Wars, and the End of the Cold War.* New York: Simon & Schuster, 2000.

Eric Foner. *The Story of American Freedom.* New York: W. W. Norton, 1998.

Thomas M. Franck and Edward Weisband. *Foreign Policy by Congress.* New York: Oxford University Press, 1979.

Charles Fried. *Order and Law: Arguing the Reagan Revolution.* New York: Simon & Schuster, 1991.

Charles Fried. *Modern Liberty and the Limits of Government*. New York: W. W. Norton, 2007.

David Frum. *Dead Right*. New York: Basic, 1994.

Francis Fukuyama. *The End of History and the Last Man*. New York: Free Press, 1992.

Francis Fukuyama. *America at the Crossroads: Democracy, Power, and the Neoconservative Legacy*. New Haven, CT: Yale University Press, 2006.

David R. Gergen. *Eyewitness to Power: The Essence of Leadership*. New York: Touchstone, 2000.

Mark Gerson, ed. *The Essential Neoconservative Reader*. Reading, MA: Addison-Wesley, 1996.

Nathan Glazer. *Remembering the Answers: Essays on the American Student Revolt*. New York: Basic, 1970.

Jonathan Glover. *Humanity: A Moral History of the Twentieth Century*. London: J. Cape, 1999.

Barry M. Goldwater. *The Conscience of a Conservative*. Shepherdsville, KY: Victor, 1960.

Barry M. Goldwater. *The Conscience of a Majority*. Englewood Cliffs, NJ: Prentice-Hall, 1970.

C. C. Goldwater, ed. *The Conscience of a Conservative*, by Barry M. Goldwater. New York: Princeton University Press, 2007.

Robert A. Goldwin and Art Kaufman, eds. *Separation of Powers—Does It Still Work?* Washington, DC: American Enterprise Institute, 1986.

Amy Gutmann. *Identity in Democracy*. Princeton: Princeton University Press, 2003.

David Halberstam. *The Fifties*. New York: Villard, 1993.

Stefan A. Halper and Jonathan Clarke. *America Alone: The Neoconservatives and the Global Order*. New York: Cambridge University Press, 2004.

Friedrich Hayek. *The Constitution of Liberty*. Chicago: University of Chicago Press, 1960.

Friedrich Hayek. *The Road to Serfdom*. London: G. Routledge & Sons, 1944.

Godfrey Hodgson. *The World Turned Right Side Up: A History of the Conservative Ascendancy in America.* Boston: Houghton Mifflin, 1996.

Eric Hoffer. *Working and Thinking on the Waterfront, a Journal, June 1958– May 1959.* New York: Harper & Row, 1969.

Eric Hoffer. *The True Believer: Thoughts on the Nature of Mass Movements.* New York: Perennial, 1989.

Richard Hofstadter. *The American Political Tradition and the Men Who Made It.* New York: Knopf, 1973.

Stephen Holmes. *Passions and Constraint: On the Theory of Liberal Democracy.* Chicago: University of Chicago Press, 1995.

John Hospers. *Libertarianism: A Political Philosophy for Tomorrow.* Los Angeles: Nash, 1971.

Michael Ignatieff. *The Lesser Evil: Political Ethics in an Age of Terror.* Princeton: Princeton University Press, 2004.

Peter Irons. *War Powers: How the Imperial Presidency Hijacked the Constitution.* New York: Metropolitan, 2005.

Josef Joffe. *Überpower: The Imperial Temptation of America.* New York: W. W. Norton, 2006.

Gordon S. Jones and John A. Marini, eds. *The Imperial Congress: Crisis in the Separation of Powers.* New York: Pharos, 1988.

Jack Kemp. *An American Renaissance: A Strategy for the 1980s.* New York: Harper & Row, 1979.

Russell Kirk. *Enemies of the Permanent Things: Observations of Abnormality in Literature and Politics.* New Rochelle, NY: Arlington House, 1969.

Russell Kirk. *The Conservative Mind: From Burke to Eliot.* 7th ed. Washington, DC: Regnery, 1995.

Russell Kirk. *Redeeming the Time.* Wilmington, DE: Intercollegiate Studies Institute, 1996.

Jeane J. Kirkpatrick. *Dictatorships and Double Standards: Rationalism and Reason in Politics.* New York: Simon & Schuster, 1982.

Irving Kristol. *Neoconservatism: The Autobiography of an Idea.* New York: Free Press, 1995.

Irving Kristol. *On the Democratic Idea in America.* New York: Harper & Row, 1972.

Richard Labunski. *James Madison and the Struggle for the Bill of Rights.* Oxford: Oxford University Press, 2006.

Lewis H. Lapham. *The Wish for Kings: Democracy at Bay.* New York: Grove, 1993.

Seymour Martin Lipset. *American Exceptionalism: A Double-Edged Sword.* New York: W. W. Norton, 1996.

Theodore J. Lowi. *The End of the Republican Era.* Norman: University of Oklahoma Press, 1995.

Pauline Maier. *American Scripture: Making the Declaration of Independence.* New York: Knopf, 1997.

Michael Mandelbaum. *The Case for Goliath: How America Acts as the World's Government in the Twenty-First Century.* New York: Public Affairs, 2005.

Thomas E. Mann, ed. *A Question of Balance: The President, the Congress, and Foreign Policy.* Washington, DC: Brookings Institution, 1990.

Thomas E. Mann and Norman J. Ornstein. *The Broken Branch: How Congress Is Failing America and How to Get It Back on Track.* New York: Oxford University Press, 2006.

Harvey C. Mansfield Jr. *America's Constitutional Soul.* Baltimore: Johns Hopkins University Press, 1991.

Jack F. Matlock Jr. *Reagan and Gorbachev: How the Cold War Ended.* New York: Random House, 2005.

Elaine Tyler May. *Homeward Bound: American Families in the Cold War Era.* New York: Basic, 1988.

David G. McCullough. *1776.* New York: Simon & Schuster, 2005.

Louis Menand. *American Studies.* New York: Farrar, Straus, & Giroux, 2002.

Robert W. Merry. *Sands of Empire: Missionary Zeal, American Foreign Policy, and the Hazards of Global Ambition.* New York: Simon & Schuster, 2005.

Frank S. Meyer. *The Conservative Mainstream.* New Rochelle, NY: Arlington House, 1969.

John Micklethwait and Adrian Wooldridge. *The Right Nation: Conservative Power in America.* New York: Penguin, 2004.

John Stuart Mill. *On Liberty and Other Essays*. Edited with an introduction and notes by John Gray. Oxford: Oxford University Press, 1998.

Martha Minow. *Not Only For Myself: Identity, Politics, and the Law*. New York: New Press, 1997.

Alan Mittleman, ed. *Religion as a Public Good: Jews and Other Americans on Religion in the Public Square*. Lanham, MD: Rowman & Littlefield, 2003.

Herbert J. Muller. *Freedom in the Modern World*. New York: Harper & Row, 1966.

Diana Mutz. *Hearing the Other Side: Deliberative versus Participatory Democracy*. Cambridge: Cambridge University Press, 2006.

George H. Nash. *The Conservative Intellectual Movement in America, Since 1945*. New York: Basic, 1976.

Michael Novak. *The Universal Hunger for Liberty: A Surprising Look Ahead at the Culture, Economics, and Politics of the Twenty-First Century*. New York: Basic, 2004.

Joseph S. Nye Jr. *Soft Power: The Means to Success in World Politics*. New York: Public Affairs, 2004.

Rick Perlstein. *Before the Storm: Barry Goldwater and the Unmaking of the American Consensus*. New York: Hill and Wang, 2001.

Nelson W. Polsby. *How Congress Evolves: Social Bases of Institutional Change*. Oxford: Oxford University Press, 2004.

Jack N. Rakove. *Original Meanings: Politics and Ideas in the Making of the Constitution*. New York: Knopf, 1996.

Jean François Revel. *Anti-Americanism*. Translated by Diarmid Cammell. San Francisco: Encounter, 2002.

James C. Roberts. *The Conservative Decade: Emerging Leaders of the 1980s*. Westport, CT: Arlington House, 1980.

Judith Rodin and Stephen P. Steinberg, eds. *Public Discourse in America: Conversation and Community in the Twenty-First Century*. Philadelphia: University of Pennsylvania Press, 2003.

Clinton Rossiter. *Conservatism in America*. New York: Knopf, 1956.

William A. Rusher. *The Rise of the Right*. New York: William Morrow, 1984.

John Samples, ed. *James Madison and the Future of Limited Government.* Washington, DC: Cato Institute, 2002.

Michael J. Sandel. *Democracy's Discontent: America in Search of a Public Philosophy.* Cambridge, MA: Belknap, 1996.

Michael J. Sandel. *Liberalism and the Limits of Justice.* 2nd ed. Cambridge: Cambridge University Press, 1998.

Charlie Savage. *Takeover: The Return of the Imperial Presidency and the Subversion of American Democracy.* New York: Little, Brown, 2007.

Arthur M. Schlesinger Jr. *The Imperial Presidency.* Boston: Houghton Mifflin, 1973.

Arthur M. Schlesinger Jr. *The Cycles of American History.* Boston: Houghton Mifflin, 1986.

Robert Schuettinger, ed. *The Conservative Tradition in European Thought: An Anthology.* New York: Putnam, 1970.

Peter Schweizer. *Reagan's War: The Epic Story of His Forty-Year Struggle and Final Triumph over Communism.* New York: Doubleday, 2002.

Stephen C. Shadegg. *Barry Goldwater: Freedom Is His Flight Plan.* New York: Fleet, 1962.

John Shattuck. *Freedom on Fire: Human Rights Wars and America's Response.* Cambridge, MA: Harvard University Press, 2003.

Anne-Marie Slaughter. *A New World Order.* Princeton: Princeton University Press, 2004.

Herbert Spencer. *The Man versus the State: With Four Essays on Politics and Society.* Edited with an introduction by Donald MacRae. Harmondsworth, UK: Penguin, 1969.

Irwin Stelzer, ed. *The Neoconservative Reader.* New York: Grove, 2004.

Jessica Stern. *Terror in the Name of God: Why Religious Militants Kill.* New York: Ecco, 2003.

Geoffrey Stone. *Perilous Times: Free Speech in Wartime from the Sedition Act of 1798 to the War on Terrorism.* New York: W. W. Norton, 2004.

Andrew Sullivan. *The Conservative Soul: How We Lost It, How to Get It Back.* New York: HarperCollins, 2006.

James A. Thurber, ed. *Rivals for Power: Presidential-Congressional Relations.* Lanham, MD: Rowman & Littlefield. 2006.

Ludwig von Mises. *Human Action; A Treatise on Economics.* New Haven, CT: Yale University Press, 1949.

Ludwig von Mises. *Socialism; An Economic and Sociological Analysis.* New Haven, CT: Yale University Press, 1951.

Christine Todd Whitman. *It's My Party, Too: The Battle for the Heart of the GOP and the Future of America.* New York: Penguin, 2005.

Sean Wilentz. *The Rise of American Democracy: Jefferson to Lincoln.* New York: W. W. Norton, 2005.

Alan Wolfe. *Does American Democracy Still Work?* New Haven, CT: Yale University Press, 2006.

Tom Wolfe. *Radical Chic and Mau-Mauing the Flak Catchers.* New York: Farrar, Straus, & Giroux, 1970.

INDEX